VIOLENCE AND NON-VIOLENCE IN THE SCHOOLS

VIOLENCE AND NON-VIOLENCE IN THE SCHOOLS

A Manual for Administration

Christine J. Villani
and
Colin C. Ward

Mellen Studies in Education
Volume 55

The Edwin Mellen Press
Lewiston•Queenston•Lampeter

Library of Congress Cataloging-in-Publication Data

Villani, Christine J.
  Violence and non-violence in the schools : a manual for administration / Christine Villani and Colin C. Ward.
      p. cm. -- (Mellen studies in education ; v. 55)
  Includes bibliographical references and index.
  ISBN 0-7734-7611-3
  1. School violence--United States--Prevention--Handbooks, manuals, etc. I. Title: Violence and nonviolence in the schools. II. Ward, Colin C. III. Title. IV. Series.

  LB3013.3 .V54 2001
  371.7'82'0973--dc21

                                                                00-064561

This is volume 55 in the continuing series
Mellen Studies in Education
Volume 55 ISBN 0-7734-7611-3
MSE Series ISBN 0-88946-935-0

A CIP catalog record for this book is available from the British Library.

The Edwin Mellen Press   The Edwin Mellen Press
Box 450   Box 67
Lewiston, New York   Queenston, Ontario
USA 14092-0450   CANADA L0S 1L0

The Edwin Mellen Press, Ltd.
Lampeter, Ceredigion, Wales
UNITED KINGDOM SA48 8LT

Printed in the United States of America

Dedication

This book is dedicated to our families (Kevin and Mathew) and (Laurie) as well as to all the devoted practitioners understanding the need to develop a "new order of things" in how we supervise in educating our youth.

Table of Contents

List of Illustrations

Acknowledgements

The authors would like to acknowledge the following people for making this book possible:

- Dr. Bonnie Mullinix, Millicent Fenwick Research Professor in Education and Public Issues at Monmouth University for her editing and review of our work.

- Dr. Linda Lyman, Associate Professor at Illinois State University for her support and review of our work.

- Dr. Lee Gray, Associate Professor at Winona State University for his support and review of our work

- The graduate students of Bradley University, Spring 1998 enrolled in Supervision and Evaluation of Instruction and Foundations of School Guidance, this is where the idea was born.

- The staff of Edwin Mellen Press for their belief in our work and assistance in our endeavors.

Introduction

Our idea for this book was formulated in the Spring of 1998. We were both professors at Bradley University in Peoria, IL. Colin with his doctorate in counseling taught the School Counseling Foundations course and Chris with her doctorate in educational leadership taught the Supervision and Evaluation of Instruction Course. Initially our discussions surrounded the topic of supervision in both fields. As we talked it became apparent to us that the field of educational leadership and the field of counseling had something to offer in terms of supervision models. We began to see the deficits in both fields and concluded that a synthesized model was called for.

Additionally, we concluded that school counselors appeared to operate as separate entities within schools being assigned the responsibility of tending to the emotional and behavioral needs of students. Whereas, administrators focused on "academics" and the effectiveness of teachers as measured by tests. Counseling supervision was premised on the emotional and behavioral needs of students and administrative supervision was premised on the behavioral aspects of teachers in the academic learning process of students. The two worlds had not met and we discovered a way to make that happen. This led to the development of our model for supervision, so named, Synthesized Professional Supervision Model. However, something was still lacking, the context. After further collegial discussions we realized that schools narrowly defined academics in terms of content area. Schools, we realized, are more than this. Our concept of academically healthy schools was derived. Still, we needed a forum to test our beliefs and newly created models.

So, in the spring of 1998 we boldly went forward and decided to collaboratively teach and create a unique collaborative assignment. We jointly planned and co-taught three class sessions with our classes in School Counseling

Foundations and Supervision and Evaluation of Instruction and planned a joint assignment for our students.

In learning teams consisting of both school counselor and educational leadership trainees, the culminating product was the development of an Academic Health Portfolio.. There were four teams for a total of 16 students. The purpose of this portfolio was to provide a context for understanding the roles of administrators and counselors and the process involved. The project rested on the assumption that clinical supervision and counseling have similarities and differences that can be integrated into a holistic paradigm that provides for a healthy academic environment for students, teachers, counselors, specialists, and non-certified staff. Therefore, the portfolio represented those theories and activities that contribute and promote the overall academic health of students. In reference to this learning project, Academic Health was defined as those dynamics contributing to the learning process of students. This involved emotional, academic, familial, cultural and administrative processes related to the students learning experience.

The creation of this portfolio required groups to meet several times and addressed the following sections:

Section 1- Supervisory Theory- Groups developed a theory for supervising teachers, school counselors, specialists and other personnel. Operating as a team, the task was to develop this theory as it related to the academic health of students and the school.

Section 2- Data Collection- Each individual in the group was required to collect data that demonstrated support for the collective theory. Each individual shadowed a school administrator and a school counselor for a half day. Diligent notes were taken regarding the activities of the administrator and counselor so that it could be related back to their developing theory. Each individual based on discussion with the team collected data from a second source. This second source consisted of interviews with teachers, students, parents and community members.

There were also additional observations of classroom instruction, faculty meetings, and board meetings, as well as, documentation reviews of the mission and goals of a school.

Section 3- Reflection- Each group wrote a collective and individual reflection on the relationship of the observational data to the supervisory theory. The individual reflection consisted of the students unique response related to the process of this project and their field of study. Part of the reflection included individual statements as to this experience and it's influence on their future role as administrators and school counselors. The final portion of the reflection piece included a linking metaphor that assisted in synthesizing the entire portfolio together.

We were excited with the results and anxious to share our work with others. We began to seek publication of our work but were met with comments such as "you can't merge these two fields, no one will listen." Being undaunted by these reactions we began to present the Synthesized Professional Supervision Model and our concept of Academically Healthy Schools at local and national conventions. The responses from practicing educators and counselors was more than encouraging. We were told that our model was needed and the lack of synthesis within our public schools was evident. We continued to work on our model presenting it to whomever would listen and instructing it in our classes despite the fact that we both moved on to other universities. Yet, it still seemed narrow to us. We were premising our concept of academically healthy schools on the belief that a synthesized supervision model between administrators, teachers, and counselors would lead to the school environment we envisioned.

It was the horrific incident at Columbine High School on April 12, 1999 that made us discover the missing link. While at the American Educational Research Convention in Montreal, Canada and over coffee we became immersed in the issue of school violence. We discovered our passion for this issue and realized that school violence could be reduced by creating academically healthy schools. It was then that we realized that our model of supervision had to encompasses the entire school community. It was not just a model for administrators to use with faculty but was a model that teachers and counselors needed to use with students. It was a fluid model that needed to encase the entire school community. We were energized and ready to move forward. We also knew that "selling" our newly formulated concepts would be difficult but we were determined. We kept writing, talking, presenting until someone heard us, Mellen Press and we are grateful for their accepting response.

Therefore, what follows is our contribution to America's schools. This book presents to you an understanding of school violence and what is meant by academically healthy schools. It then discusses in complete theoretical detail the various models of supervision in both fields. Following this complete documentation you are presented with our model of supervision and a demonstration for its utilization in creating academically healthy schools that can lead to a reduction of school violence. We close the book with a chapter called "Metaphorically Speaking," as a harmonious means to making this new and challenging concept worth doing as well as focus questions to determine how academically healthy your school is.

Reese M. House[1]

The authors of this book have addressed the difficult issues of educating today's students in the changing landscape of America. Clearly, the opportunity to achieve success in school in a safe environment is the ultimate goal of our educational system. However, the two worlds of academic success and safety often clash. This book provides a possibility for changing the system to reduce violence and increase the success of students. This is not an easy task, and the authors present here a complex and sometimes intellectual approach to systemic change. They admit that they don't have all the answers, but they provide a map that is very much worth exploring.

The essence of their approach is the belief that a fluid supervisory model needs to be implemented in every school community. The school community is a key point. It is not possible to address change unless we address the context in which the school exists. Too often schools are isolated and alienated from parents and the community. This must change and the supervisory model explained here offers some hope. Key elements of this proposed model include the concept that the curriculum implemented in the school and the methods used in teaching must be integrated and that teachers need to spend more time understanding how students learn rather than all of their time on the standards and curricula. All members of the school community are key players in this model and must work collaboratively and collectively to establish a school climate of "academic health" for success and integrity.

The book provides a theoretical model and approach that allows leaders in school to undertake such a change process. The change implies a paradigm shift in how schools are organized. It means that all employees of the school, all students, all parents and all community members are important to the academic health of the school. If this model can remove barriers to academic success by

---

[1] Dr. House, a program specialist at The Education Trust in Washington DC, is a former school counselor and professor emeritus of counselor education at Oregon State University, Corvallis, Oregon.

changing how we work in schools, or even if it has the slightest potential to remove these barriers then we are obligated to pay attention.

Integral to this model is reflecting on the process and status of education in classrooms, in schools and in communities. With the crisis of the moment at hand in every school in America, the immediate challenge is to find the time to reflect. But, first all staff members need to understand the importance of this reflection and be taught how to do it. The ideas presented emphasize that critical self-reflection represents the essence of transformational learning. Extensive professional development will be needed to teach all school personnel the self-reflection methods needed for successful implementation.

The authors suggest that the lack of a systemic change model is what keeps schools maintaining the status quo. I agree, and we can no longer maintain the status quo is schools. It is time for change. This model moves from an adversarial model to a collaborative systemic approach to change, and for this reason alone, it is worth considering for integration into the training and practice of educational leaders.

Chapter 1
Academic Health

The Principal of Columbine High School in Littleton, Colorado was quoted as saying "we had no idea." Like others, he was baffled why two seniors, viewed by staff as being free of academic or behavior problems, would implement a massive murder-suicide.

As a country, how do we make sense of the surge of violence in America's schools that have led to such a multitude of shootings? The blame has been indiscriminately placed on the all-to-common culprits: gun control, the media, parents, educators, and funding agencies. Despite the veracity of the complaint, the problem still remains – schools in conjunction with their communities need to do something. The question is "what?"

The rate of violent acts committed by juveniles is reaching epidemic proportions. Antisocial behavior in children and adolescents is prevalent in 30 - 50% of clinical referrals across all demographic areas in the United States (Kendall, Reber, McLeer, Epps, & Ronan, 1990). Juvenile homicides have increased five times faster in the past five years than have homicides committed by adults (Lang, 1991), and risen 61% during the 1980s (National Coalition of State Juvenile Justice Advisory Groups, 1993). Even patterns of truancy, lying, alcohol and drug abuse, deliberately annoying others, verbally and physically threatening others, suicide threats and attempts common in schools across America all have one thing in common – aggression. A further question is "why?"

Often normal conditions of adolescence, such as, hypervigilance, timidity in expressing an opinion, inability to set goals, acting out behaviors, and lower intelligence are factors associated with children and adolescents predisposed to aggressive tendencies (Studer, 1996). These young individuals tend to be fearful of strange places and have difficulty taking risks and establishing goals. They struggle to feel good about themselves, unable to predict positive outcomes in the activities occurring around them and, most importantly, perceiving themselves as distant and apart from peers and adults alike.

Aggressive and violent student behavior is highly correlated with poor school involvement and community adjustment (Henry, Stephenson, Hanson, & Hargett, 1993). As Durkheim proported in 1951, these are students poorly integrated in society. Research points to two predominant systems impacting the development of these characteristics: the family and the media. Outside of the military and law enforcement agencies, the family is considered to be the most violent institution in society (Myers, 1993). Furthermore, the media provides a desensitizing barrage that might actually promote aggressive behaviors in children (Myers, 1993). These forces are illustrated in the microcosm of a school community where children and adolescents struggle with identifying with themselves and with others. In addition to the already overwhelming pressures placed on schools for addressing the academic needs of its students, schools must find a way to connect itself with these children of trauma. The question is "how?"

American schools have the mistaken belief that a child with good grades, no major discipline problems and good attendance is ultimately "fine." This is often not the case and illustrated by how students with a strong achievement orientation (high grades, participation in athletics, class clown, most popular, etc.) often struggle with poor self-esteem and suicidal ideation. When academics focus on the acquisition of "content," the emotional, familial, and cultural values and ethics of the student and school communities are sacrificed. These values are central to the individual and social development of students. As Gardner (1993) asserts, they represent areas of intelligence ignored by the vast majority of our country's teaching institutions. School programs on anger control strategies, assertiveness training, problem solving, and conflict mediation are first steps in violence prevention.   Like a band-aide on an open wound, they can do little however to promote healing in the face of a spreading infection.

As a community of educators, an academic environment that promotes self-esteem and self-efficacy in students is desperately needed. We propose that a majority of today's schools are academically unhealthy and unable to either recognize or address the dynamics inherent with school-related aggression and violence. This book takes an in-depth look at the issues of school violence and the need for creating academically healthy environments. We propose that, in order to accomplish this, the link to academically healthy schools lies in the supervision of the entire school community. To be academically healthy, schools must promote those dynamics contributing to the learning process of their students. This involves the emotional, academic, familial, cultural, and administrative processes related to students' learning experiences.

We propose a model of supervision that is both fluid and dynamic from administrator to faculty member, administrator to student, and faculty member to student where the relational, developmental, reflective, and cultural themes of learning and change are addressed. It views the supervisory relationship as a "vehicle for learning" (Eckstein & Wallerstein, 1972) and for teaching schools to teach students to feel accepted and connected to themselves and others. In essence, it teaches educators and students to be more humane than the forces impacting them. This model of supervision is the base for creating academically healthy schools and a systemic step toward the reduction and, hopefully, elimination of school violence.

The book will also present case scenarios for application of the model and ends with a contract asking schools to commit to becoming academically healthy. In addition, a series of reflective questions for assessing the schools level of academic health and how to begin the process of promoting academic health are included.

Academically Healthy Schools

Academically healthy schools represent those dynamics that contribute to the learning process of students. These dynamics include the emotional, academic, familial, cultural and administrative processes related to the student's experiences. An overload in any of these areas will impact on the learning process of students. Academically healthy schools allow for and integrate these dynamics in all aspects of the school experience for all members· of the school setting. They are reflected in the mission, values, and relationships where the emphasis of how the curriculum is implemented is as important as what the curriculum is. Furthermore, academic health is founded on the interdependent nature of learning emphasizing an open rather than closed educational environment. Davis (1976) distinguished open from closed systems by explaining, "Closed systems are totally isolated from and independent of their environment; they are static, predictable, and ultimately tend towards a state of equilibrium, stillness, inactivity. An open system is defined as an exchange of matter with its environment, importing and exporting energy, building up and breaking down its own component parts" (p.281). By embracing the complex interconnectedness between students, administrators, faculty and schools can resist the temptation toward entropy and create open learning environments where individuals thrive, reason, and change themselves within an interactive context.

Academically healthy schools allow for a dynamic process between all members in an effort to improve and increase learning and growth for all. It is an ongoing collaborative process between and among administrators, faculty, staff, students and parents. It requires a high level of communication skills and the building of interpersonal relationships. Mutual trust must be established in a climate of fairness and integrity that allows for risk taking on the part of all members.

Academically healthy schools allow for a give and take relationship that encompasses the strengths as well as the weakness of its members. Within an academically healthy school students are fostered to exhibit behaviors that indicate positive attitudes and enthusiasm toward peers, faculty, staff, administrators and academic pursuits. Faculty, staff, and administrators are also encouraged to exhibit behaviors that are positive toward one another, students, parents, the community at large and their own professional growth.

Academically healthy schools encourage students to achieve to their highest potential and are able to demonstrate the knowledge and skills through various means of assessment. Faculty, staff, administrators, and parents are involved in the on going process of curriculum instruction and assessment. Community members are encouraged and enlisted to support these endeavors.

Academically healthy schools have an overall mission and value and belief system that embodies the academic, familial, cultural, and administrative processes designated as paramount to the individual school community. Academically healthy schools create these dynamics through a model of supervision that enables all of its members to have their needs met. A school's ability to effectively promote student and adult learning and self growth is related to the above dynamics coupled with a supervision model that allows for these dynamics to occur.

Academics- Historical Perspective

Thomas Jefferson has long been credited as one of the major forerunners and proponents of the common school. Jefferson believed firmly in the education of all for the betterment of the citizenry of society. It was through his efforts and the efforts of others like Horace Mann that led to the creation of the public school system we have today. Jefferson viewed education as the foundation of democracy and viewed ignorance as a destructive force to self-government. He believed that only enlightened people could take the responsibility for a democratic government. Jefferson believed that there were no limits to the amount of knowledge one could acquire. He believed that humans were inherently good but needed to be educated. Universal schooling would produce a mass of good citizens. His belief was that elementary schools were to provide the instruction in reading, writing, arithmetic, geography, and the values of being a good citizen. He believed that elementary schools were more important than universities because it was safer to enlighten all people than a few from highly learned institutions. In 1818, Jefferson listed six objectives for primary education (as cited in Peterson, 1960):

- To give every citizen the information he needs for the transaction of his own business
- To enable him to calculate for himself, and to express and preserve his ideas, his contracts, and accounts in writing.
- To improve, by reading, his morals and faculties.
- To understand his duties to his neighbors and country, and to discharge with competence the functions confided to him by either.
- To know his rights, to exercise with order and justice those he retains, to choose with discretion the fiduciary of those he delegates; and to notice their conduct with diligence, with candor and judgement.

And, in general to observe with intelligence and faithfulness all the social relations under which he shall be placed. For Jefferson, education was the foundation for happiness, prosperity, and good government.

Another proponent of Jefferson's philosophy was Horace Mann. Mann's Twelfth Annual Report written in 1858 is considered the most comprehensive report advocating common schools. Mann related public education to many things including; social progress, civic issues, moral education, pedagogy, reading, music, and discipline. Mann's arguments regarding social progress, and moral education serve as an historical base for academically healthy schools.

Imagine, the concept of academically healthy schools being purported back in 1858!. With regard to social progress Mann stated:

> Education, then, beyond all other devices of human origins, is the great equalizer of the condition of men-the balance-wheel of social machinery...It does better than to disarm the poor of their hostility towards the rich, it prevents being poor...The spread of education by enlarging the cultivated class or caste, will open a wider area over which the social feelings will expand; and if this education should be universal and complete, it would do more than all things to obliterate factitious distinctions in society. (Mann, 1848, 87-89).

Mann's most poignant statement that demonstrates the need for creating schools that are academically healthy is stated in his argument for moral education.

> Moral education is a primal necessity of social existence. The unrestrained passions of men are not only homicidal but suicidal; and a community without a conscience would soon extinguish itself. Even with a natural conscience, how often has Evil triumphed over Good! From the beginning of time, Wrong has followed Right, as the shadow substance. As the relations of men became more complex, and the business of world more extended, new opportunities and new temptations of wrong-doing have been created...For every lock that is made, a false key is made to pick it; and for every Paradise that is created, there is a Satan who would scale its walls...Against these social vices, in all ages of the world the admonitions of good men have been directed...and yet the great ocean of vice and crime overleaps every embankment, under our feet, and sweeps away securities of social order, of property, liberty and life...But to all doubters, disbeliveers, or despairers, in human progress, it may still be said, there is one experiment which has never yet been tried...Its formula intelligible to all; and it is as legible as though written in starry letters on an azure sky... Train up a child in way he should go, and when he is old he will not depart from it. But this experiment has never yet been tried. Education has never yet been brought to bear with one hundredth part of its potential force, upon then natures of children, and through them upon the character of men and of race...(Mann, 1948, 98-101).

The origin of recognizing academic health as the enlightenment of the whole child lies in the early foundation of public education. It emphasized moral development, basic values of right from wrong. It meant addressing self-esteem and self-efficacy within the context of family and community. The emphasis on pedagogical content at the expense social consciousness not only reinforces the isolation and detachment felt by many students leading to violence and aggression, but undermines the intent and purpose of what it means to educate today's youth. Finally, academic health means understanding that the self does not develop in isolation, but is impacted by broader systemic and social processes influencing mental health and achievement. School leaders, therefore, need to be provided with eco-systemic competencies, that emphasize working with students in view of the interacting developmental, social and cultural factors influencing their learning and ability to solve problems. This is the essence of supervision for promoting and creating academically healthy school environments.

Chapter 2

Violence in Schools: An Academically "Unhealthy" Environment

Violent crimes among juveniles have been rapidly increasing since the mid-1980's. Generally, race and gender, have been cited for the reason in juvenile involvement with crime. However, age has now become a major factor. Between 1985 and 1992 the number of homicides committed by young people and the number of homicides they committed with guns has doubled. The increases have been linked to the availability of guns and the increase in illegal drug use among juveniles (Blumstein, 1995).

Prior to 1985 individuals age 18-24 were the most likely group to commit murder. Since 1985 the homicide rate rose to over 138 percent between the ages of 16 and 18. In the the past seven years, since 1992, there has been a steady increase of homicides in the age group of 11-16. The surge in violent juvenile crime coincides with many things including the increase of drug use and the availability of guns.

Guns are increasingly utilized in homicides among juveniles. From 1976-1985, a gun was used in approximately 59 percent of homicides involving juveniles ages 10-18. By 1992 the number of juvenile murders had doubled. Juveniles' use of guns is more random than adults. Bravado, impulsivity, recklessness, and demonstrations of power mark teenage behavior; as opposed to adults who generally show more restraint. Differences once settled by fist fights have escalated to shooting incidents (Blumstein, 1995).

Geoffrey Canada in his book "Fist, Stick, Knife, Gun," (1995) poignantly states in the preface of his book our countries historical love for violence:

> America has long had a love affair with violence and guns. It's our history; we Teach it to all our young. The Revolution, the "taming of the West," the Civil War, the world wars, and on and on. Guns, justice, righteousness, freedom-Liberty-all tied to violence. Even when we try to teach about non-violence, we have to use the Reverend Dr. Martin Luther King, Jr. killed by violence...

Canada who was raised in the South Bronx, an inner city ghetto, reflects on how things changed from the use of fists to guns. In his preface he states:

> I don't know if this is true or not, but I've watched children grow up fighting with guns, and now their young adults. The next generation might be called the Uzi generation because of their penchant for automatic weapons. These children, armed better than police, are growing up as violent if not more so than the handgun generation. And the gun manufacturers in their greed continue to pump more and more guns into our already saturated ghettos.

The availability and advertisement of guns clearly exaggerate violence among adolescents. This is complicated by the interrelated dynamics between poverty and gang activity where children living in poverty feel powerless. As children of trauma, this feeling of powerlessness leads to the flourishing of criminal activity in these environments. Juveniles living in poverty have few role models or job opportunities, which appears to escalate criminal activity. Criminal activity makes them feel powerful and adds excitement, status, and financial gain.

It is estimated that over 5,000 gangs exist nationally in this country. Over a quarter of a million juveniles have membership in gangs. There is a reward for juveniles who belong to gangs; it provides identity, purpose, and a sense of self-worth. Gangs also offer protection, camaraderie, and excitement to young people. The violence in gangs is further glorified through the lens of media. In addition television, radio, film, publications, music glorify violence. According to the Center for Media and Values (1993), children watch an average of 28 hours of television weekly. Approximately five violent acts per hour occur in prime-time programming. Yet, television, movies, music, and publications mirror the society we live in. Violence sells.

Bernardine Dohrn (1997), Director of Children and Family Justice Center in Chicago, IL states that realities are two fold: children are killing children and guns are the instrument or agent driving the youth homicide statistic. Dohrn points out that between 1984 and 1994 youth homicide soared. The number of children charged with killing another child rose over one hundred and forty-four percent. The United States has seventy-five percent of child murderers in the industrialized world. Additionally, the number of youth homicides using a gun began to rise in 1984 and has more than doubled since then. Gun homicide is the second leading cause of death for young people.

Over the past decade school violence has increased and not just in terms of homicide. The problems of violence include physical conflicts among students, robbery, vandalism, and verbal abuse of teachers coupled with student drug and alcohol abuse, and possession of weapons. In the past decade each one of these areas has escalated to a level of severity that seems difficult to manage. The problem does not exist solely in urban settings but has extended to suburban and rural. Because of the growing intensity of violence, public schools are becoming less and less safe.

Within an increasingly violent social context, schools are under funded and ill equipped to meet the educational and social needs of the students. This is due in a large part to the fact that schools are being asked to meet a variety of demands within their local communities along with providing the basics of an education. Jonathan Kozol in his book "Savage Inequalities" states that on top of the under funded and ill-equipped facilities that create an obstacle to learning students are experiencing more and more violence in schools. This violence is not limited to urban areas. If anything, the rise of violence is in suburban areas. Kozol points out that no school is immune to violence, regardless of its location or wealth.

The statistics are astounding:

- School violence has increased over the past five years in nearly 40 percent of America's city and towns.
- In 1990 one out of 25 high school students carried a gun, by 1998 it almost doubled.
- Over 135,000 guns are brought to school every day.

Many schools are taking preventive measures to reducing violence. Schools have engaged in conflict resolution and peer mediation programs that are included in their curriculum. Schools have developed "drug free" "gun free" and "fight free" policies. In addition, schools have raised their expectations regarding behavior whereby violence is not an acceptable behavior. So then why is violence still on the rise?

According to Dohrn (1997) it is because we have not taken the specific steps necessary to make a difference. Dohrn states that we need to take eight basic steps:

1. Treat all children as children by recognizing their developmental needs
2. Resist the criminalization of students by making teaching opportunities out of a child's behavior. Involve them in peer mediation, teen courts, and mentoring.
3. Create smaller safer schools.
4. Remove guns form the environment by removing them from the local community
5. Create neighborhood alternatives to costly and failing incarceration
6. Create mentoring programs
7. Advocate for hopeful future
8. Listen to children.

Berreth and Berman (1997) would say that Dohrn's ideas cannot work unless we first establish moral dimensions to schools. Citing the philosophy of Amitai Etzioni, Berreth and Berman propose that in order to promote character education empathy and self-discipline must first be encouraged. Empathy allows the child to appreciate the perspective and feelings of another, to sense violation of justice and to distinguish between right and wrong. Self-discipline is the ability to take action and delay or forego gratification to remain committed to a set of values or goals.

As a foundation to moral behavior, empathy and self-discipline need to be nurtured in students. With a focus on basic decision making skills, students can learn how to delay gratification, set positive values, learn how to act responsibly while being provided opportunities to test these skills with peers and adults. However, doing the above requires establishing a moral school community. A moral school community is one that celebrates moral values, exemplifies positive moral values among adults, and functions as a hub for the neighborhood community. In establishing itself as a moral school community then students are aided in developing problem solving, conflict resolution skills, and decision-making skills. This leads to the appreciation of diversity within the school community.

The major possibility may reside in how intervention programs often fail to address how every member of the school community is responsible for reducing violence and determining whether their school is academically healthy. This may represent a new paradigm attempting to empower the children of trauma with opportunities for emotional and social growth in substitution of violence, drug use, and gang membership. By definition, empowerment is the process where, "obstacles are removed.... a chance is given....one is entrusted or sent on a mission" (adapted from the American Heritage, 1998). This implies a paradigm for schools that engenders a context whereby obstacles are removed to enable students the opportunities for change, learning, and problem solving. Furthermore, a trusting and supportive social atmosphere is established committed to the change and developmental growth of everyone. The essence of empowerment, therefore, is collaboration, commitment, and trust in the goals pursued by students, faculty, and administration. Academic health is founded on these principles and central to effective supervision.

Academically Healthy Schools and Violence

As stated in Chapter 1, academically healthy schools are schools whose dynamics contribute to the learning and problem-solving process of students. This involves the emotional, academic, familial, cultural, and administrative processes related to students' experience. The quality of a student's experience is interdependent on his/her interaction with administrators and staff. This is a circular process and based on a belief in the circular causality of interactions (Bateson, 1956). In relation to linear reasoning where A causes B, circular causality argues that A, B, and C interact to cause D. From a circular perspective, school problems are a collective rather than just a sum of influence by the participating factors (social, familial, academic, developmental, etc.). Understanding the wholeness of a school community assists in viewing every problem (i.e. violence) in it's context and in relation to all other parts of the system rather than an effect in response to a specific cause (i.e. media). The responsibility of enhancing academic health of students lies with parents, faculty, administration, school board/community members and the quality of their interaction to empower it's members to thrive, reason and grow.

Starratt (1993) quotes Machiavelli as writing, "There is nothing more difficult to take in hand, more perilous to conduct, or more uncertain in its success, than to take the lead in the introduction of a new order of things" (p. 2). The integration of a systemic paradigm into the instruction of students and supervision of faculty requires more then commentary. It calls for transformational leadership to bring about a change in fundamental attitudes, perceptions, values, and commitments from others. Burns (1978) indicated that this type of transformational leadership seeks to unite people in the pursuit of communal interests beyond their individual interests and to call attention to the basic purpose of the organization and the society it serves.

Youth violence in schools is an extreme extension of unhealthy academic school environments. Academically healthy schools create environments where every member of the school community is growing intellectually, psychologically, physically, and spiritually. To introduce a "new order of things" school leadership needs to embody the systemic qualities representative of academically healthy institutions. John Gardner (1990) echoed this in his characteristics of leaders as those individuals who a) think long term beyond the immediate problems, b) look beyond the agency or unit they are leading in order to grasp its relationship to larger realities of the organization as well as the external environment, c) reach and influence people beyond their jurisdiction, d) emphasize vision, values and motivation; they intuitively grasp the non-rational and unconscious elements in the leader-constituent interaction, e) have political skills to cope with conflicting requirements of multiple constituencies, and f) never accept the status quo; they always think in terms of renewal.

Empowered by healthy environments, all in the school can feel safe, secure, and cared for; where they are perceived as, "...active creators and definers of their realities, not passive respondents or victims of environmental circumstance" (Tricket et al, 1994). Leadership in an academically healthy school emphasizes the importance of understanding how individuals construct their world through social exchange processes (Trickett et al, 1994). "The degree to which a given form of understanding prevails or is sustained across time", echoed Gergen (1985), "is not fundamentally dependent on the empirical validity of the perspective in question, but on the vicissitudes of social process (e.g. communications, negotiation, conflict, rhetoric)" (p. 268). This further implies clear boundaries where the rules and mission of the school are understandable and roles and responsibilities of each member are emphasized and supported. Within this "matrix identities" articulating a clear structure while understanding the reciprocal nature of growth can assist in promoting a sense of belonging as well as autonomy. It is this structure that provides a net of safety for encouraging the risk taking necessary for change that goes well beyond course content and curriculum.

Although violence in schools can be viewed as an extension of social forces related to an overall increase of youth violence nationwide, a systemic paradigm focused on increasing the academic health of schools can provide a preventative rather than just a responsive learning environment. Understanding the wholeness of how members influence one another can assist in adopting a new paradigm of school leadership for empowering the emotional, psychological, familial/cultural, and academic/professional dynamics of change representative of academic health. It is not change, or the pace of change, that is adversely effecting our educational environments and many teachers psyche, it is the lack of a systematic change process (Merickel, 1995). Change is a process, not a destination. Without a process for change, this situation can lead to chaos. In an era of high stakes testing where student health lies invisible behind test scores, the time for thinking about and initiating change is now. The following questions are useful to consider as schools and school leaders begin to introduce a "new order of things" for enhancing the level and quality of academic health of their students and staff. They are:

- What are the steps of change needed to promote academic health?
- Are the steps of change large enough to move the system forward, but small enough to be accomplished?
- What resistance will need to be prepared for when the unexpected develops?
- How will the vision of the organization (school) need to be shifted to identify all members in relationship with one another?
- How well do the operations, curricula, and learning materials coincide with the vision and goals of developing and maintaining an academically healthy environment?

□ How will the structure and roles of the school organization need to be adjusted and reassigned so that administration, faculty, staff and students can develop with the speed that non-stop change requires?

□ How will systematic time outs be built into the schedule to better manage the constant stress of non-stop change?

The pursuit of understanding the complexity of academic health and applying its principles to the leadership of school organizations, patterns of violence can be reduced and students can be empowered with opportunities for change. It is this profound belief in the process and preparation of change that encompasses the following model of supervision that will assist in creating academically health environments.

Chapter Three

The Synthesized Professional Supervision Model:
Principles of Change

Educational leadership presupposes that traditional learning theories developed for student education is applicable to enhancing and facilitating professional practice. Grounded in behavioral assumptions, educational supervision has maintained an authoritative stance in requiring supervisees (i.e. teachers) to develop in accordance with the worldview of supervisors (i.e. administrators). Although recent approaches to supervision, namely the clinical supervision model, identifies practitioner development as important to professional growth, it is absent of a supervisory pedagogy. This creates a vacuum in which supervisors in educational settings resort back to their own training model; that of behaviorism. By perceiving relationships as processes of task analysis, the development of models specific to the supervision process and supervisee development were dramatically impeded. Management rather than collaborative supervisory practices, therefore, have not only historically defined the interrelationships between administration and faculty but also has been consistent in how instruction has been communicated to students.

Although various models have been proposed to assist supervisors in conceptualizing the unique dynamics of counselor development it has done little to provide opportunities for supervisee skill enhancement, self-awareness and integrated professional and personal identity related to the roles and tasks of professionals. The Synthesized Professional Supervision Model is presented as an 'introduction of a new order of things' where the reciprocal processes of professional practice, supervisee development, the supervisory relationship, and the reflective cycle are coupled with professional growth. It provides a framework for working with educational professionals across a myriad of disciplines. Moving beyond the behavioral models of educational learning that has perpetuated the field since the 1960's, this book articulates a model of supervision that synthesizes a) supervisory reflective cycles, b) supervisee developmental stages, c) influencing supervisee paradigms and d) phases of professional supervision in relation to professional practice. Furthermore, this model contends that supervisee development occurs concurrently with the progression of the supervisory relationship. It is focused on transforming supervisee dissonance into professional schema's through a reflective cycle of supervisor-supervisee interaction. In contrast to performance models of supervision, the pedagogical interventions posed by this model allows the supervisor to enhance the professional growth of supervisees by remaining cognizant of supervisee development and the influencing paradigms upon professional growth. The principles of reflective learning rather than behaviorism provide a foundation that enables the model to cross a myriad of disciplines and address supervision as a process for improving professional practice (see figure 1).

Kuhn (1970) writes that when a paradigm is either shifted or expanded to new areas, new problems arise that lead to the proposal and development of new paradigms. The evolution of the SPSM is grounded in a paradigm shift from linear causality to nonlinear mutual causality in viewing professional development and student learning. The words of John Weakland (1990) provide a challenge for this shift of paradigms to approach supervision and change; "....we must make a fresh start; in effect, to construct a new myth, a new view of problems and their resolution that is minimally constrained by past myths" (p.107). A constructivist and developmental framework to management (leadership) and supervision of educators opens the door to a variety of interrelated systemic learning theories that have been ignored in the face of positivistic education. Even the word *constructivism* illustrates this function. It is based on the verb *construct* meaning "to form or build; to create by systematically arranging ideas or terms" (American Heritage Dictionary, 1992). The Latin translation, stemming from the word *construe,* is more to the point when it simply states "to pile up."

Figure 1. Overview of the Synthesized Professional Supervision Model

Supervisory Reflective Cycle of Professional Interaction	Supervisee Stages of Professional Development	Paradigms influencing Professional Practice	Phases of Professional Supervision
Disorienting Professional Experience	SELF CENTERED	REFLECTIVITY PARADIGM	CONTEXTUAL ORIENTATION
Supervision Relationship	CLIENT CENTERED	LEARNING SYTLE PARADIGM	ESTABLISHING TRUST
Supervisor Intervention	PROCESS CENTERED	CULTURAL PARADIGM	CONCEPTUAL DEVELOPMENT
Shift in Supervisee Perception and/or Behavior and Reemergence to the Professional Context	CONTEXT CENTERED	PEDAGOGY PARADIGM	CLINICAL INDEPENDENCE

The following section is a "piling up" principles related to history of supervision and learning theories illustrating a chain evidence for guiding the emergence and essence of the Synthesized Professional Supervision Model (SPSM). The four guiding principles of *Interdependency, Person over Performance, Professional Growth is Developmental,* and *Supervision is a Nonlinear Process* provide guidance to better understanding the SPSM in working with administrators, educators, students, and families in and outside of schools. To address violence in schools is to address the context in which it can be preventative: interdependent relationships of human interaction.

Guiding Principle One: Interdependency

Although a supervision model has no direct power to make changes or implement programs it is in a position to influence feedback loops associated with school related problems. General systems theory argues that the whole is qualitatively different from the sum of the system's individual elements (Simon et al., 1985). Change in one part of a system (individual, group, organization, etc.) is followed by compensatory change in other parts of the system (Bowen, 1966). Wheatley (1994) highlighted this point by emphasizing that the "part" is the whole. Any action of any part can manifest transformative change to the whole. Furthermore, when the tendency for a certain direction is established, the feedback will increase this tendency (Harth, 1982). An open system orients toward disequalibrium feeding on fluxes, perturbations, and anomalies to create a feedback loop positive for reorganization and "morphogenic" change. Davis (1976) further distinguished open from closed systems by explaining, "Closed systems are totally isolated from and independent of their environment; they are static and predictable, and they ultimately tend towards a state of equilibrium, stillness, inactivity. An open system is defined as an exchange of matter with its environment, importing and exporting energy, building up and breaking down its own component parts" (p.281).

With a supervision model that emphasizes interdependency, empowerment, and reflectivity, teachers will be more inclined to create an open environment where ideas are shared, debated, and uniquely constructed within the relationships of learning. This systemic orientation focuses on the interactive qualities impacting administration, faculty, students, and families in defining and maintaining the problem (i.e. violence). The intention of the SPSM, therefore, is to facilitate the system (school) toward a change in interaction. It emphasizes the reciprocal and interdependent impact of school boards on administrators, of administrators to the teaching and counseling faculty, and of the faculty to the students and parents. It is comprised of four primary dynamics: 1) the relational, 2) developmental, 3) the reflective, and 4) the cultural themes of learning and change. The intention of the Synthesized Professional Supervision Model is to assist in the enhancement of academically healthy schools: leading to the reduction of school violence.

Sergiovanni and Starratt (1993, 1998) provide a distinct paradigm that emphasizes the interdependent and reciprocal nature of the supervision relationship. Recognizing that supervision had been defined by extrinsic criteria and based on the scientific management theory of people like Frederick Taylor, Sergiovanni and Starratt articulated an approach to supervision focused on the intrinsic moral quality of the professional. In relation to educational instruction, they indicate that since teaching is a caring profession that respects the integrity for what is taught, not to do so would be a violation to the profession. Supervision, therefore, needs to be an interactional activity that provides support while furthering the caring relationship between the teacher and student.

Moral supervision postulated that duties and obligations come from shared values, ideas, and ideals held by both the supervisor and supervisee. The relationship is viewed as reciprocal and interdependent where the supervisee responds to shared commitments and interdependent values with the supervisor. Within the field of education the concept of moral supervision allows for schools to be transformed from organization to communities. Supervision is centered on shared values, beliefs, and commitments. Supervisors identify explicitly their values and beliefs. These values and beliefs shape the supervisor's behaviors and make it possible to promote collegiality and a morally driven interdependence between the supervisor and the supervisee. Supervisors do not have to rely on external controls since supervisees respond to their duties and obligations due to this moral interdependence. Furthermore, supervision rests on the concern for what things mean notjust the way things look. As stated by Sergiovanni and Starratt (1998):

> The metaphors phonetics and semantics can help this distinction. Tending to supervisory and teaching behaviors as they appear on the surface is an example of the phonetic view. It does not matter so much whether the supervisor is involved in leading, coaching, managing evaluating, administering, or teaching. If the emphasis in these activities is on the looks and sounds of behavior, on the form or shape that this behavior takes as opposed to what the behavior means to teachers and students, the view is phonetic (p. 49).

From this perspective moral supervision is hierarchically independent and role-free where the interaction is not dictated or shaped by the structure of the organization. It is a set of ideals and skills that can help supervisees function more effectively that allows for collegial supervision, mentoring supervision, as well as informal supervision. Doing rewarding work rather than being extrinsically rewarded for work that gets done fosters motivation.

Moral supervision rests on intrinsic motivation and the belief that people have shared values and beliefs that foster their desire to work and grow as professionals. Moral supervision moves completely away from the models previously addressed. The work of Sergiovanni and Starratt clearly takes into account the basic tenet of professional practice, that of morals. This emphasis on person over and in relation to performance is in stark contrast to the historical onset and emergence of educational leadership and supervision.

Guiding Principle Two: Person over Performance

Two major theories that strongly influenced supervisory practices are scientific management and human relations theory. Scientific management theory has its roots in the work of Frederick Taylor during the early 1900's. Taylor's belief hinged on the factory model of supervision during the Industrial Revolution. His form of scientific management included careful observations and task analysis. His belief was that once workers had the appropriate equipment their job was to be compliant and do as they were told. Individual thinking was strongly discouraged. Therefore, the scientific management method included creating a work system utilizing the most appropriate resources, communicating expectations to workers, training workers, and monitoring and evaluating carefully to ensure full compliance. Although scientific management is autocratic and efficient it clearly discourages individuality and creativity (Callahan, 1962).

Elton Mayo, in the 1930's, countered this with his theory of human relations supervision. Mayo believed that workers could improve their productivity if their social needs were met He theorized that workers needed to be treated decently, be involved in the decision making process, and be allowed to interact among their peers. His ideals of prioritizing the person over his/her performance proved to be both successful and a challenge to the scientific method (Mayo, 1933). As with many paradigm shifts that dramatically shift from the status quo, supervisors gradually resorted back to performance and a scientific style to management.

The next significant shift toward a person centered supervision model emerged in the 1960's, combining the views of scientific management and human relations to create the human resource theory of supervision. Leading proponents and developers of this theory included Warren Bennis, Chris Argyris, Douglas McGregor and Renis Likert. Human resource theory is premised on the belief that human beings need to demonstrate competency, commitment, and responsibility to be an active and viable member of the organization. Therefore, supervision from this framework focused on creating a supervisory context of support rather than autocratic guidance (Argyris, 1967). Douglas McGregor (1960) theory of supervision and management categorized these two competing positions of management as Theory of X and Y. Theory X applied to traditional or scientific management while Theory Y applied to a human resource approach to management (see figure 2).

Figure 2. Overview of Theory X and Y

Theory X	Theory Y
❑ The average person has an inherent dislike for work and will avoid it when possible; ❑ The average person lacks ambition, wishes to avoid responsibility and wants security above all other things; ❑ The average person is self-centered and resistant to change; ❑ Most people must be coerced, directed, and threatened with punishment to get them productive; and ❑ The average person is gullible and not very bright.	❑ Work is as natural as play or rest; ❑ People will demonstrate self-direction and self-control in the service of objectives to which they are committed; ❑ The average person learns, under proper conditions, to accept and seek responsibility. The average person is motivated. It is the job of management to ensure that people recognize and develop these characteristics for themselves; ❑ People have a relatively high degree of imagination, ingenuity, and creativity; and ❑ It is management's responsibility to arrange the organization so that people can achieve their goals best by directing their own efforts toward the goals and objectives of the organization.

McGregor pointed out that every supervisory act illustrated an intentionality of action that rested one of these two competing principles. He summed up his theory in this way:

> Theory X leads naturally to an emphasis on the tactics of control-to procedures and techniques for telling people what to do, for determining whether they are doing it, and for administering rewards and punishments. Since an underlying assumption is that people must be made to do what is necessary for the success of the enterprise, attention is naturally directed to the techniques of direction and control. Theory Y, on the other hand leads to a preoccupation with the nature of relationships, with the creation if an environment which will encourage commitment to organizational objectives and which will provide opportunities for the maximum exercise of initiative, ingenuity, and self-direction in achieving them (1960, p.132).

The polarity introduced by McGregor continued through the 1970's where educational supervision was viewed either from a management approach (scientific and clinical) or more humanistic (collegial and self-directed). However, the 1980's ushered in a changing climate in schools. With increased enrollment, schools were called upon to move into a third-party role to manage services in a time of declining resources (i.e. special services, multiculturalism and diversity). Increased attention was placed on being accountable to the subject matter at the expense of shifting developmental, familial, and social influences. A new view of supervision developed known as "neo-scientific management". In many respects, this was in reaction to the human relations theorists and shifting climate in schools. Neoscientific management rests on control, efficiency, and accountability. It renewed the interest in closely supervising supervisees. The focus on standardization created an impersonal atmosphere. Educators were held accountable through the used of norm-referenced tests given to students for measuring their "growth". The degree to which their students scored high on these forms of evaluation has become the determination for their ability to perform their duties (Sergiovanni and Starratt, 1998).

Grounded on behavioral models of change, educational leadership began emphasizing an external model of efficiency and performance rather than on the intrinsic value on human relations where person-hood was valued over, and in relation to, performance. This dichotomy of management defined the perception of professional growth and current models of educational supervision. Although there are an array of supervision frameworks that attempt to address the needs of supervisees, the current emphasis on scientific management and behavioral pedagogy is inherent in their delivery. As Kuhn (1970) articulated, initial changes in professional paradigms represent a similar intentionality with a shift in language and perception only. It emphasized an attitude of "of look how different this is" while maintaining the status-quo. While supervisors stress cooperation, service, and democracy most still lean on behavioral approaches to changing people.

Guiding Principle Three: Professional Growth is Developmental

The formalized process of supervision began when England's Royal College of Physicians supported a law that deemed the death of a patient by an "unlicensed practitioner" a felony. Apothecaries, who at the time were treating the large mass of poor, were thus pressured to seek the "opinion" of a physician. This dialogue of a "superior to an inferior" (Thomas Percival, 1803, as cited in Kaslow, 1977) became further rooted in clinical supervision with the founding of the AMA in 1847 and the emergence of psychiatry in the 1920's. Although this new "specialty" grounded supervision within a medical paradigm, it also opened the way for the extrapolation of emerging learning theories to the supervisory experience. Behavioral, social learning and competency-based training frameworks approached supervision from tenets espoused by their theoretical orientation. The operating paradigm in educational leadership, therefore, presupposes that traditional learning theories developed for student education is applicable to enhancing and facilitating professional practice. As stated earlier, the inherent intentionality of current educational supervision, grounded in behavioral assumptions, has maintained an authoritative stance in requiring supervisees (i.e. teachers) to develop in accordance with the worldview of supervisors (i.e. administration, school board).

This dynamic prompted the use of applying competency-validated instruments to the study of supervision. Thus, methodological enmeshment not only restrained the development of supervision as a profession, but assumed that variables of change between the two disciplines (supervision/teaching) were identical. Although these "supervision models" intended to aid in the interpretation of complex phenomena and assist the supervisee in learning complex skills, it provided few directions for either research or practice.

This limitation was initially addressed in the field of counseling supervision which, similar to educational supervision, utilized "counseling-bound" paradigms of supervision. With Russell's (1984) assertion that the supervisors did not practice supervision as they practiced counseling, and that the interactional characteristics of supervision were uniquely different from that of a counseling interview (Holloway, 1994), cross theoretical models of supervisee development emerged (Stoltenberg, 1981; Loganbill, 1982; Blocher, 1983; Stoltenberg & Delworth, 1987; Skovholt, 1993). They described a sequential, hierarchical process of counselor development and related tasks as well as matching supervisor interventions for each stage. A growing body of research supported the general tenets of developmental models (Borders, 1989; Tracey, 1989; Rabinowitz, 1986; Heppner, 1994). Of these, none has had a more systematic impact on supervision literature and research than Stoltenberg's (1981) Counselor Complexity Model. Described as the "most heuristic model to date" (Worthington, 1984, p. 63), it integrated Hogan's (1964) stage approach to supervision with Hunt's (as cited in Stoltenberg & Delworth, 1987) conceptual systems theory as applied to learning environments. The counselor is portrayed as progressing through a sequence of four identifiable stages while addressing issues of autonomy, self-awareness, and the acquisition of skills and related theory. Furthermore, trainees are characterized as anxious and dependent while confronting aspects of motivation, learning needs, and dynamics of resistance. Eight growth areas (skills, assessment, interpersonal, conceptualization, individual differences, theoretical orientation, treatment goals/plans, and professional ethics) are additionally outlined as a trainee develops conceptual understanding related to their role as a professional and the counseling process.

Watkins (1995), in his exhaustive review of recent developmental literature pertaining to counseling supervision, summarized the impact of developmental models in the definition of supervision as a unique and complex process. He concluded that:

a) The majority of studies found some degree of support for developmental models or a dimension of supervision.

b) Perceptions of both supervisors and supervisees were broadly consistent with developmental models.

c) Beginning supervisee were generally found to be more in need of structure, direction.

d) Advanced, as opposed to beginning supervisees were found to generally need less structure, direction, and guidance and be more willing to consider their own personal issues and their effect on therapy.

e) Some research showed that, with experience, supervisees' needs changed in developmentally appropriate ways and that, over time, supervisees showed increases in developmentally relevant structures (i.e. self and other awareness, autonomy, and motivation).

Literature on the developmental nature of supervision articulated that the supervisor should have a range of styles to assist the counselor's movement through these definable stages (Littrell et al., 1979; Stoltenberg, 1981; Loganbill et al., 1982; Yogev, 1982; Stoltenberg & Delworth, 1987). Accordingly, a supervisor who recognized the strengths and learning styles of supervisees could better create an appropriate learning environment (Wiley & Ray; 1986). The need for support and greater structure at the beginning levels of training is in contrast to mature supervisory relationships characterized by supervisee autonomy and personal inquiry (Holloway & Nuefeldt, 1994). Hawkins and Shohet (1989) presented a synthesis of Stoltenberg & Delworth's (1987) complexity model of counselor development while articulating a context for which the supervisor can modify his/her approach to definable trainee developmental stages. Hawkins & Shohet (1989) outlined four stages of supervisee development and corresponding supervisor approach styles paying particular attention to self-and-other awareness, motivation, and autonomy (see figure 3)

Figure 3. Supervisee Development

LEVEL ONE (Self Centered) *Novice*   Supervisee Characteristics   High levels of anxiety associated with performance and evaluation anxiety leading to patterns of *dependency* on supervisor. Enters with little insight and is focused on general skill performance and has difficulty attuning to thematic patterns or the overview of the learning and counseling process. This may make them impatient.   Matching Supervisor Approach   Provide a clear and structured approach that provides positive feedback and encouragement (affective relational components).
LEVEL TWO (Client Centered) *Journeyman*   Supervisee Characteristics   Fluctuation between dependence and autonomy; and between over-confidence and being overwhelmed Although less simplistic, supervisee oscillates between excitement and anger/depression with increased reactance to the interactional triangle (self, supervisor and client).   Matching Supervisor Approach   Although less structured and didactic the supervisor will need to contain the emotional reactivity accompanied with growing professional independence. The supervisory relationship acts as a "container" for encouraging increased autonomy and process-

> focused observation.

LEVEL THREE (Process Centered)   *Independent*
Supervisee Characteristics
Exhibits increased professional self-confidence, with only conditional dependency on the supervisor. Increased insight beyond specific skills, and in observing thematic patterns (wider context--*systemic*) in client(s) can adjust his/her approach to meet the presenting needs.
Matching Supervisor Approach
Supervisory relationship is more collegial in matching trainee's growing independence and comfort with increased autonomy in the interactional triangle. Supervision is characterized by sharing and exemplification augmented by professional and personal confrontation.

LEVEL FOUR (Process-in-Context Centered) *Master craftsman*
Supervisee Characteristics
Trainee has developed into an integrated practitioner characterized by personal autonomy, insightful awareness, personal security, stable motivation and awareness of need to confront his or her own personal and professional problems.
Matching Supervisor Approach
The supervisor interacts in a collegial and collaborative style providing an atmosphere for the counselor to explore and reflect on complex interactions of their professional practice with others and related variables of the thematic dimensions of the therapy process. Utilizing self disclosure, the supervisor is supportive and encouraging of this independent growth and learning process of the supervisee

Clinical Supervision Model

The rational for developmental supervision rests on the premise that supervision needs to match the supervisee's developmental levels, expertise, and commitment to their job. Goldhammer (1969), and subsequently Glatthorn (1990), provided early educational supervision models that implied a focus contrary to traditional behavioral management models focused on professional development as eventually outlined in the work of Glickman, Gordan & Gordan (1985; 1990; 1995; 1998).

Robert Goldhammer (1969) presented a model of supervision encouraging a face to face relationship between the supervisor and supervisee. He concluded that most supervision models were conducted at a distance and that a face to face relationship would allow supervision to be "up close." The intent of the clinical supervision model was to improve instructional techniques and assist in the professional growth of the supervisee. Goldhammer (1969) further provided a distinction between supervision and evaluation. He viewed evaluation as only a single facet of the clinical supervision model whereas clinical supervision represented an ongoing process designed to foster professional development and improve teaching practices. He states in his book Clinical Supervision: Special Methods for the Supervision of Teachers the following:

> I mean to convey an image of face to face relationships between supervisors and teachers. History provides the principal reason for this emphasis, namely, that in many situations presently and during various periods in its development, supervision has been conducted as supervision from a distance, as, for example, supervision of curriculum development or of instructional policies framed by committees of teachers. "Clinical" supervision is meant to imply supervision up close (p.54).

He also conceptualized clinical supervision as circular in design defined by three distinctive phases. Phase one explored the supervisee's concerns regarding his/her instruction within mutual process whereby goals for improving instruction as well as self-improvement were established. The second phase is observation, not evaluation, where the supervisor collect s data based on the agreed upon goals. The final phase is a feedback conference where the supervisor provides objective observational data to the supervisee. The supervisor and supervisee cooperatively analyze the data and reach agreement as to what is happening. Cooperatively, the teacher and the supervisor make decisions regarding future actions and procedures. The feedback process naturally provides for the next planning conference.

Keith Acheson and Meredith Gall (1980, 1987, 1992 and 1997) have used and researched the clinical supervision model extensively. They summarize the essential characteristics as follows:

1. To improve instruction (performance), supervisees must learn specific intellectual and behavioral skills.
2. Supervisors should take responsibility for helping supervisee's develop: skills for analyzing the instructional process based on systematic data, skills for experimentation and modification, and obtaining skills for building a wider range of instructional skills and techniques.
3. The aim is improve performance not change personalities.
4. The planning phase focuses on making and testing hypothesis based on observational data.
5. The conference deals with only a few issues that are amenable to change.
6. The feedback conference is constructive. It reinforces successful patterns and looks to change unsuccessful ones.
7. It is based on observational data not unsubstantiated value judgments.
8. The cycle of planning, observation, and feedback is continuous and cumulative.
9. Supervision is a dynamic process of give and take. It is a collegial relationship.
10. Supervisees have the freedom and responsibility to initiate issues, analyze and improve their own performance and develop personal styles.
11. The supervisory process is primarily centered on the analysis of performance.

12. Supervisors have both the freedom and the responsibility to analyze and evaluate their own supervision in a manner similar to the supervisee's analysis and evaluation of their performance.

The overall goals of clinical supervision are to, a) provide supervisee's with objective feedback to the current state of their performance, b) diagnose and solve instructional problems, c) develop skill in using instructional strategies, d) evaluate for purposes of promotion, tenure, or other decisions, and e) help the supevisee develop a positive attitude about continued professional development (Acheson and Gall, 1997). Clinical supervision is an intensive and interpersonal relationship where the supervisor oversees the development of the supervisee. This development of the supervisee entails professional knowledge, skill, confidence, objectivity and interpersonal interactions designed to improve competency and effective delivery within the supervisee's professional field. Furthermore, Clinical supervision conceptually is a helping relationship. It is most effective when supervisors and supervisee's share trust, openness, and honesty the supervisors are still responsible for administrative evaluation (Knoff, 1988).

The clinical supervision model is premised on the concept of a partnership. It goes beyond evaluations, although evaluation is a piece of the model. The supervisor facilitates the teacher throughout the process of setting goals, analyzing observational data, and making effective changes based on the data. Acheson and Gall (1997) articulate that the clinical supervision model and being "interactive rather than directive, democratic rather than authoritarian, teacher centered-rather than supervisor-centered. This supervisory style is called clinical supervision," (p. 9).

Instructional Supervision Model

Allan Glatthorn (1990) synthesized theory, research, and practice with equal weight given to each and created the model for instructional supervision. He grounded his model practice as it related to theory and research. Glatthorn began by reconceputalizing the clinical supervision model. In his critiques of the clinical supervision model Glatthorn stated the following: the clinical supervision model lacks a theoretical perspective, the clinical supervision model focuses on the development of teacher skills, the model is inflexible, and the supervisory cycle does not make sufficient provision for conceptual development and skill instruction. Glatthorn then developed what he considers to be a theoretical framework for a reconceptualized clinical supervision model. His basic theoretical premise is as follows:

1. The primary purpose of supervision is to improve student achievement by facilitating the professional growth of the teacher.
2. The primary means for reaching the goal is to enable the teacher to direct and accomplish his or her own professional growth.
3. Teaching is a craft, art, and science.
4. There is no single best way to teach.
5. The optimal supervisor-supervisee relationship is collegial and collaborative.
6. Supervision is primarily concerned with development, not evaluation.
7. The supervisor and teacher should adopt a broad perspective that is sensitive to the multifaceted influences affecting teaching.
8. Teachers are unique individuals with varying developmental needs.
9. Supervision is a value-laden pursuit, one in which ethical action is a base requisite.

Based on this framework Glatthorn reconceptualized the model of clinical supervision as the base for his instructional supervision model. There are three portions to the reconceptualized clinical supervision model. First the reconceptualized model is self-directed by the supervisee.   Second, the model is multiple in its process.   Glatthorn refers to modules instead of stages or phases because his modules can be used in a variety of sequences (see figure 4).

Figure 4. Glatthorn's Professional Development Modules

Module	Explanation
Taking-stock conference	A conference held at the beginning of the year, at the end or at any time to develop the supervisory relationship, assess general progress, plan activities and give the supervisor feedback
Diagnostic observation	An observation done with wide lens approach. Data is collected to help the supervisor and supervisee analyze classroom interactions and identify problems.
Analysis of teaching	Process focuses on understanding a teaching episode by analyzing observational data. It is done independently and cooperatively.
Debriefing conference	Held after an observation to continue the analysis of teaching and share results of the analysis.
Knowledge development conference	Conference held whenever deemed necessary to share and strengthen the knowledge base, develop long and short term instructional plans, and improve decision making skills.
Instructional support	Conference held whenever necessary to work on assessing and improving instructional supports systems.
Student analysis	Conference held whenever necessary to work together on assessing student performance, student behavior, student motivation, and to plan an interventions.
Coaching	Conference held when necessary using a coaching approach to improve teaching skills.
Focused observation	Observation conducted with narrow lens, observer collects data on single pre-determined aspect of classroom interactions.

Informal Observation	A brief-drop in visit made periodically throughout the year to monitor performance, reinforce effective behaviors and become aware of potential problems.

Glatthorn contended that the use of these modules influenced teacher professional development due to their flexibility. He stated that these modules allowed for free flowing rational movement that encouraged supervisee development while taking into consideration their developmental needs. Glatthorn further conceptualized clinical supervision model within a differentiated system of interaction. He viewed differentiated supervision as allowing supervisee's to choose the types of supervisory services they received. It is premised on the fact that supervisee's are professionals and that teaching is a profession. Glatthorn's model provided for three choices of professional development: a) intensive development, another term for the clinical supervision model, b) cooperative development, a process where a small team of supervisee's work together to facilitate their own professional growth, and c) self-directed development, a process where the supervisee identifies a developmental goal, finds the needed resources and works toward completing that goal.

Differentiated supervision allows for meeting the needs of all supervisee's. It takes into account the novice, passive, marginal, and productive supervisee. Rather than locking all supervisee's into one model, the differentiated model is organized to meet the needs of the supervisee based on level of experience and need.

Motivation and Professional Development

Maslow (1954) developed a framework for understanding human motivation that has been the foundation of motivational research for many years. Maslow's premise was that there is a hierarchy of needs that motivate human to act in a certain manner. There are five stage to Maslow's hierarchy of human needs: physiological needs, safety, belonging and love, esteem, and self-actualization. Each are discussed below.

> Physiological needs- Maslow states that the initial motivation is to satisfy biological demands for food, water, sleep, and exercise. Until these needs are satisfied humans are not motivated to do anything else.
>
> Safety- After the physiological needs are satisfied, humans are motivated to obtain the nice things of human life. A comfortable, regulated environment is sought. Security, stability, dependency and rules eliminate fear and anxiety. A person is motivated to seek shelter in a familiar location with a secure source of income.
>
> Belonging and love- After safety needs are satisfied an individual seeks involvement with others as group members and as a partner. The individual desires affection with friends and family, acceptance with group members of different organizations and affiliations, and the love and affection of a partner.
>
> Esteem- At this level the individual seeks to become a contributing and leading member of the group. The individual wishes to be admired and viable. The person will take action, assume leadership, and help others. The individual feels competent and valued by the group.
>
> Self-actualization- Once all the previous needs have been satisfied motivation at this level is based on an individual's own standards. The individual follows what he or she believes is best, regardless of what other's think. Being true to one's own inclinations becomes the mark of self-actualization.

Glickman et al (1998) posited their developmental supervision model on the above theory of motivation with one caveat; the critical aspect of choice. According to Glickman et al the developmental supervision model must provide choices to the supervisee with regard to their professional development. The issue of choice illuminates from the motivational work done by people like Deci (1975, 1982) and DeCharms (1968, 1976). Their work validated the work of Maslow but added the critical determinant of choice with regard to motivation and professional growth. DeCharms and Deci demonstrated that when given choices individuals would work hard at a task they chose without the promise of an extrinsic reward such as money or time off. Their work countered the work of people like Skinner who based motivation on extrinsic stimulation and the need for external forces to motivate humans to completing a task.

Based on the above Glickman et al (1998) postulates that developmental supervision rests on the motivational theory of choice. Understanding a supervisee's stage of cognitive, conceptual, moral, and ego development assists the supervisor in guiding a supervisee to an appropriate level of supervision. In other words, the supervisor becomes informational rather than controlling. The supervisor by understanding the supervisee's developmental levels has the tools to inform the supervisee as to the level of supervision best fits the supervisee's needs. However, the supervisee makes the choice as to the form of supervision he or she feels most comfortable with. By allowing choice, the developmental supervision model fosters motivation for supervisee growth.

The developmental supervision model sets it pedagogy on cognitive, conceptual, ego, and moral development. Based on this the developmental supervision model posits its implementation on motivational theory with a focus on choice. It's concept of motivational theory as a means to effective supervision has merit. However, the process of supervision goes well beyond motivation and choice. It is a complex process that may incorporate various aspects of developmental supervision but also includes many facets of human existence within the realm of professional practice.

Contending that supervision is a unique process and dependent on the developmental and experiential level of the supervisee, developmental theories to educational leadership emerged. Glickman, Gordan & Gordan (1985, 1990, 1995 & 1998) have fostered the majority of the work on developmental supervision. Glickman et al. place supervisees within three different developmental stages; low, moderate, and high developmental levels.

Supervisees at the low developmental stage are described as operating at a concrete operational stage of cognitive development. They are described as having low conceptual levels and moral reasoning that is at the preconventional level. In addition, they lack self-adequacy and are at a fearful stage of ego development. Supervisees at this stage are described as being unable to define problems, respond to problems, and unable to make decisions. At this stage direct supervision is indicated. Glickman et al. (1998), state that supervisee's at this stage need structured, intensive, and directive supervision.

Supervisee's at the moderate developmental stages are described as functioning at the formal operations stages of cognitive development. They exhibit a conventional level of moral reasoning and function at a moderate conceptual level. Supervisee's at this level can generate some solutions to problems and operate in a collegial manner, however they still need assistance in researching all options. Glickman et al.(1998), state that supervisee's at this stage require a collaborative supervisory approach. This approach allows for the supervisee to share with other supervisee's or the supervisor perceptions regarding performance and offer possible solutions. However, the supervisee still needs the guidance and perceptions of the supervisor in order to improve performance and move to a level of independence.

Supervisee's at the high developmental stages are described as operating at the postformal operations stage of cognitive development. They exhibit high conceptual levels, post conventional levels of moral reasoning, and are at an autonomous stage of ego development. Supervisee's at this level can solve a problem from many perspectives and generate a variety of alternative solutions. They are autonomous, independent, creative, explorative, and decisive. Glickman et al (1998), state that supervision at this stage needs to be self-directed. Supervisors need to be non-directive and supportive since the supervisee's are quite capable of their own professional growth.

The developmental supervision model is based on various theories of adult development. Glickman et al (1998) discuss adult cognitive development, conceptual development, moral development and ego development. However, their model rest strongly on the various theories of motivation that are worth discussing, particularly that of Abraham Maslow.

Guiding Principle Four: Supervision is a Nonlinear Learning Process

Combs (1954), a perceptual psychologist, contended that behavior is an expression of internal impressions and completely determined to the perceptual filed of the organism. From this position, it is not the skills, which are important, but the intentions with which they are applied. Professional practice, therefore, is embodied in the practitioner's use of "self" as an instrument of change with and for others. As Calia (1974) explains, "...confining the helping process to a series of graded steps negates the importance of the inspirational and humanistic components of therapists' conditions" (p. 91). Far too often supervision and leadership is reduced to presenting a series of skills which can decontextualize the understanding and application of personal characteristics essential to instruction, counseling, and leadership. Even the connotation to skill training implies the exercise of ability without regard for the context in which it may be put to use. "To talk about salient, psychological relevant phenomena such as empathy, problem solving, or coping as if these were nothing more that skills or collections of skills" declares Martin (1990), "is more that unwarranted connotational freedom. It is inaccurate and potentially confusing" (p. 403). Learning the skills and methods of teaching, counseling, and activism, does not constitute being a teacher, counselor, and/or advocate. The general skills approach as presented in earlier chapters as the historical paradigm of supervision and leadership represents a trade-off. In its effort to maximize the number of areas its general principles apply to, this approach must sacrifice genuineness for hollow application. "It seems possible", states Mahon (as cited in Martin, 1990), "that too many trainers are making the jump from skill description to skill development without fully understanding how to more effectively complete this transition" (p. 43).

Arguably, therefore, the acquisition of professional skills is based not on behavioral reductionism, but grounded in dispositional structures of the practitioner and understanding the conceptualization of how personal characteristics of the helper may be best predictors of successful helping outcomes. By accentuating the person a move from linear to nonlinear training methodologies is clearly needed.

The recent emergence of chaos theory from the fields of mathematics and physics, introduces non-linear principles of the universe to the learning process where inherent patterns are present in seemly random and chaotic systems (Glieck, 1987). The discovery that "hidden within the unpredictability of a disorderly phenomena are deep structures of order" is central to chaos theory (Hayles, 1991). Wheatley (1994) contended that order and chaos are mirror images of one another and that learning "...is the capacity to respond to disorder with renewed life" (p.11). From this paradigm, chaos is a natural context for maturation and learning and that there are patterns of order within disorder; a paradox where "it appears on the surface as random, but contains a hidden structure or pattern of order" (Chieuw, as cited in You, 1991). Contrary to linear sequential processing, paradox is an inherent systemic process defining what Glieck (1987) terms, *sensitive dependence*: "the notion that a butterfly stirring in Peking can transform storm systems in New York" (Glieck, 1987, p.8). The unpredictability of learning and change is implied with Chieuw (1991) emphasizing that, "Sensitive dependence on initial conditions ensure that no two outcomes are alike" (p. 70).

The emphasis for supervisors and leaders to maintain flexibility in face of disorder and acceptance in face of differences. Nonlinear learning challenges instructors to understand and form quality relationships with others, to interact flexibly with complex systems and contexts, and to attain an interindividual balance in self-development (Wilber, 1995). The practitioner who is grounded in nonlinear thinking seeks to discover what is meaningful to others by "taking the big and little bits of personal history, habits, and attitudes to see how they form constructions of the world" (Carlsen, 1988, p. 100). It is also important for the trainee to be involved in critical study and personal reflection on existing psychological knowledge while attempting to cultivate and refine genuine dispositions for helping oneself and others (Martin, 1990).

For professional practitioners to reach this perspective there must be a focus on the person and the context in which they work. The acquisition of content knowledge and experience in the practice of their skills, in isolation from their personal development, is not sufficient in the preparation of effective counselors (Wilber, 1995). To engage in a supervisory, leadership, instructional, or helping relationship is a risk reciprocally taken, and experienced mutually, by both parties (i.e. instructor-student). It is entered into with the hope that change will occur and an understanding that the quality of their relationship will greatly influence it. It is often painful, chaotic, exhilarating, and joyful. To supervise practitioners for this undaunting context is an enormous challenge. To do so without emphasis on the personhood or the context in which they will work is to lessen the welfare of both trainee and client learning.

Chapter 4

The Primary Dynamics of the SPSM

As discussed in chapter three, supervision and leadership occur in relation with others that promote a reflective cycle between participants to assist in the developmental growth of supervisees. It is within this interdependent interaction, rather than the neglect of it, that outcomes for academic health will occur. Toinette Eugene (1989) articulated that the attitude of care liberates individuals from the fear that others will use gross power to seize what they want. Leadership and supervision, therefore, needs to be liberating for all people in the school setting to engender not only trust between one another, but be cognizant that being cared for may be a necessary prerequisite to learning to care. As articulated by Noddings (1991):

> Schools by themselves cannot do much to remove the crisis, but educators can begin to address the fundamental problem instead of aggravating it by promoting technical and mechanistic solutions. It may be impossible for regular schools to provide the sort of care required by children who have never experienced caring relations, but schools can help most children to learn more about how to care and be cared for, and our society ought to make education for caring a top priority (p. 166).

The following interactive paradigms of the SPSM model contend that the academic heath of students does not occur in isolation from, but in concert with one another. It is a model of supervision for understanding effective learning interactions between administrators and faculty, administrators and students, and faculty with students. The paradigms of reflectivity, learning style, pedagogy, and multiculturalism define the purpose of these interactions while presenting a framework for how caring supervisory relationships can enhance both professional development and the academic health of school settings. As outlined in figure 5, these four paradigms of influence articulate how a reflective dialogue, with deliberate pedagogical intent that matches to the learning style and multicultural worldview of supervisees, can enhance the complexity in which they "make sense" of their professional relationships (i.e. peers, students, parents).

Figure 5. The Synthesized Professional Supervision Model

Supervisory Reflective Cycle of Professional Interaction	Supervisee Stages of Professional Development	Paradigms influencing Professional Practice	Phases of Professional Supervision
Disorienting Counseling Experience Supervisee is anxious with a perceived sense of professional inadequacy.	SELF CENTERED High levels of anxiety associated with performance and evaluation anxiety leading to patterns of *dependency* on supervisor.	REFLECTIVITY PARADIGM	CONTEXTUAL ORIENTATION Supervisee experiences cognitive and emotional dissonance in adjustment to the professional climate.
Supervision Relationship Supervisor is nonjudgmental, supportive and validating.	CLIENT CENTERED Fluctuation between dependence and autonomy; and between over-confidence and being overwhelmed	LEARNING SYTLE PARADIGM	ESTABLISHING TRUST Developing a positive learning alliance is central for a supervisee's willingness to reflect on dissonant professional experiences.
Supervisor Intervention Supervisor seeks to expand supervisee conceptual complexity to	PROCESS CENTERED Exhibits increased professional self-confidence, with increased insight beyond specific	CULTURAL PARADIGM	CONCEPTUAL DEVELOPMENT Promoting advanced conceptual complexity through reflective dialogue

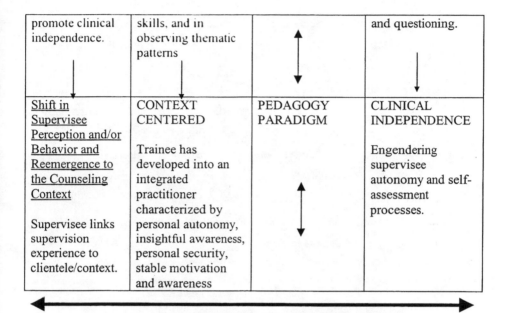

promote clinical independence.	skills, and in observing thematic patterns		and questioning.
Shift in Supervisee Perception and/or Behavior and Reemergence to the Counseling Context

Supervisee links supervision experience to clientele/context. | CONTEXT CENTERED

Trainee has developed into an integrated practitioner characterized by personal autonomy, insightful awareness, personal security, stable motivation and awareness | PEDAGOGY PARADIGM | CLINICAL INDEPENDENCE

Engendering supervisee autonomy and self-assessment processes. |

Matching Supervisory Pedagogy

Reflectivity Paradigm

Described in teacher education literature as primarily a problem-solving paradigm (Ross, 1989; Van Manen, 1977), reflective practice has been interpreted in a variety of ways (Stuessy & Naizer, 1996). First defined by Dewey (1938) as "active, persistent, and careful consideration of any belief or supposed form of knowledge in the light of the grounds that support it and the further conclusions to which it tends…" (p. 9), reflective learning is essentially the meta-management of concentration, comprehension and affect. Wilson, Shulman and Richert (1987) supported this contention and added that the reflective professional must reconstruct the events, emotions, and accomplishments of a professional experience.

Garman (1984) viewed reflection as a process that involved two basic and complementary approaches. Reflection on action is a procedure where the supervisee studies the immediate at hand events in order to understand them, learn from them, and develop skills for useful practice. Reflection on action according to Garman involved five processes: involvement in a scenario; a record of the scenario; the meaning of the data; the educational construal; and confirmations.

Involvement in a scenario involves setting aside certain events for study and reflection. The record of the scenario comes from data taken by an observer, audio or visual recording. The meaning of the data is the analysis of the data collected. This analysis allows for discoveries, interpretations, explanations, and evaluations. The educational construal allows the supervisee to put events and meanings in an abbreviated form for future use by identifying a concept or principle, noting a significant incident, or developing a conceptual framework. Confirmation allows the supervisee to determine whether the construal has meaning.

Meaningful learning occurs only through self-examination of assumptions, patterns of interactions, and the operating premises of action. Critical self-reflection, therefore, represents the essence of transformational learning. This is summarized by Tremmel (1993) who pictured reflective learning as " . . . a dance-like pattern, simultaneously involved in design and in playing various roles in virtual and real worlds while, at the same time, remaining detached enough to observe and feel the action that is occurring, and to respond" (p. 436). Schon (1987) viewed this as *knowing-in-action* and emphasizes recognition of discomfort in response to professional experiences which highlights the reflective learning process and provides a context for the critical analysis of base assumptions and beliefs about those we serve, change, and one's practice.

Providing a context that encourages supervisees to willingly explore dissonant professional experiences is the essence of a reflective supervisory relationship and necessary for professionals to shift to a higher order of conceptual processing (Mezirow, 1994). Reflective learning, as applied to practitioner development and supervision, can be defined as the process whereby trainees meaningfully reconstruct counseling experiences utilizing a repertoire of understandings, images, and actions to reframe a troubling situation so that problem solving interventions can be generated (Ward & House, 1998). In construing and appropriating a new or revised interpretation of the meaning of one's experience as a guide to action (Colton & Sparks-Langer, 1993; Mezirow, 1994), the practitioner's level of consciousness through the recognition of inconsistencies or incongruencies is increased.

Reflective learning is contingent upon the quality of the supervisory relationship (Sexton & Whiston, 1994). It is within this "constructed interaction" that active learning occurs and knowledge on how to change behavior develops (Mahon & Altmann, 1991). This implies a cyclical supervisory interaction that seeks to aid supervisees as they reflect on uncertain counseling experiences in supervision and, subsequently, reenter the counseling context with a meaningful change in perception and/or practice. The supervisory relationship becomes a container to review counselor's intentionality, belief, and base assumptions surrounding disorienting professional events.

Understanding the cyclical reflective process inherent in the supervisory relationship provides a context for the review of supervisee intentionality in clarifying patterns and themes necessary for learning and professional growth directing attention to three broad questions to be explored with the supervisee:

- How do I make sense of the dissonant or distressful experiences?

- What does this mean with regard to my professional skills, theory of change, and gaps in my professional development needing to be addressed?

- How does this assist in better understanding the world view of the administrator/teacher/student/parent?

This cyclical dynamic has previously been demonstrated through the research of Neufeldt, Karno and Nelson (1996) and Worthen and McNeill (1996).

These authors found that counseling supervision stems from a causal condition of uncertainty, which is addressed in the supervisory relationship. In this relationship, a reexamination of professional assumptions assists the supervisee in developing a metaperspective of the counseling process. As a result, a supervisor is challenged to create a learning context that enhances supervisees' skills as they construct relevant frames from which to devise effective strategies in working with clients (Holloway, 1992).

Further analysis by Ward and House (1998; 1999) identified a cyclical interactive process between supervisors and supervisees exhibited throughout the development of their on-site supervision relationship and central to relating dimensions of growth. The supervisory relationship typically began with supervisees entering supervision in a state of anxiety and perceived professional inadequacy. This state of emotional and cognitive dissonance was addressed by supervisors with a discernibly nonjudgmental, supporting, and validating stance that sought to normalize the interns' struggle. As a result, supervisees and supervisors experienced a level of trust where supervisees perceived supervision as a relational context for reflecting on dissonant internship experiences.

Supervisors then sought to expand the conceptual abilities of supervisees with the intent of promoting their teaching and counseling skills. School practitioners returned to the professional setting and experienced further disruptive learning situations. This cycle was repeated upon subsequent return to on-site supervision. As a microcosm of the larger sequence of on-site supervision, this reflective cycle served to assist school counseling interns in addressing previously uncertain school counseling internship experiences. A renewed confidence resulted and effectively invoked the learning dimensions specific to each phase of on-site supervision development and their overall supervisory experience. The SPSM links these principles of reflective learning theory to the dynamics of practitioner supervision and phases of supervision development as developed by Ward & House (1999) (see figure 6).

A sequential series of four phases of the supervision relationship has been shown to emerge over the course of supervision (Ward. 1997). Supervisory dyads progress through a series of sequential phases. These are, a) contextual orientation (orienting the supervisee to the school climate), b) establishing trust (establishing a level of trust within the supervisory relationship), c) conceptual development (encouraging advanced conceptualization processes), and d) clinical independence (promoting trainee clinical independence).

The dimensions of supervisee experience, therefore, articulate processes central to their becoming independent practitioners. The first phase of on-site counseling supervision, contextual orientation, was represented by increased levels of learning dissonance and the urgency of performance experienced in schools. Establishing trust, the second phase of supervision development, was represented by the dimensions of supervisors accessibility, support, and with practitioners. This assisted in on-site supervision progressing to the third developmental, conceptual development, which portrayed the supervisor utilizing thematic observations, reflective modeling, and illustrative examples to enhance supervisees conceptual understanding of learning and their roles as educators and counselors. This pedagogical focus was central to expanding the conceptual complexity of the interns while encouraging their independence. The final developmental phase of clinical independence focused on dimensions encouraging supervisees' self-assessment, self-generation, and professional risk taking representative of independent school professionals.

Supervisees (administrators, faculty, students) enter the school community often emotionally and cognitively overwhelmed while dependent on the supervisor for providing structured guidance and encouragement in orienting to the school climate. Through continued exposure to both the school context and related supervisory dynamics, the supervisees anxieties lessened; he/she became more independent in conceptualizing the learning process and determining areas of both professional and personal growth. The findings of Ward and House

(1999) suggest that on-site supervision provided a supportive and reassuring context for instruction to the orientation to the school context, facilitated a trusting supervisory relationship, and promoted advanced conceptual development. The development of greater conceptual complexity of practitioners provided the foundation for final phase of supervision development focused on increasing the autonomy of practitioners in both their clinical self- assessment and practice.

Figure 6. A Model of Reflective Counseling Supervision

Supervisory Reflective Cycle of Interaction ← →	Phases of Professional Supervision
Disorienting Professional Experience Supervisee is anxious with a perceived sense of professional inadequacy.	CONTEXTUAL ORIENTATION Supervisee experience of Cognitive and Emotional Dissonance in adjustment to the professional climate.
Supervision Relationship Supervisor is nonjudgmental, supportive and validating.	ESTABLISHING TRUST Experience of trust central to supervisee willingness to address dissonant internship experiences.
Supervisor Intervention Supervisor seeks to expand supervisee conceptual complexity to promote clinical independence.	CONCEPTUAL DEVELOPMENT Supervisor promoting advanced conceptual complexity through thematic and reflective dialogue.
Shift in Supervisee Perception and/or Behavior and Reemergence to the Professional Context Supervisee links supervision experience to clientele/context.	CLINICAL INDEPENDENCE Supervisor facilitates supervisee autonomy

The SPSM links these principles of reflective learning theory to the dynamics of practitioner supervision and phases of supervision development. It is our contention that whether it is contextual, conceptual or clinical, the uncertainty experienced by administrators, faculty, and students provides the learning dissonance necessary for developing advanced conceptual and clinical skills needed for educating and counseling others.

Learning Style Paradigm

Another portion of the paradigms influencing professional practice is the learning style paradigm. Although there are various learning style theories, the work of Gregoric (citation) fits the basis of supervision comprehensively. Therefore, learning styles are viewed as a matrix that encompasses four overriding styles; concrete sequential, abstract sequential, abstract random and concrete random. Gregoric developed a style matrix that assists an individual in recognizing his dominant learning style. However, Gregoric points out that life experiences, further education and knowledge can and does lead to individuals shifting their learning style. This matches our philosophy that supervision strategies fluctuate based on the learning style of the individual at that time. In other words a person who is concrete sequential may move to a balance between concrete sequential and abstract sequential based on experience and professional practice.

An overview is provided below to demonstrate to the reader the complexity of learning styles and the importance of supervision to match the learning preferences of the supervisee.

An individual whose dominant learning style is *concrete sequential* lives in a concrete, physical, and objective world. This individual views the world as static, objective, and predictable. The concrete sequential learning style approaches the world in a linear, ordered, sequential, and one-dimensional manner. The thinking process has a clear beginning and end for this individual.

Therefore, supervision requires approaching the concrete sequential learning style in a linear and ordered fashion. Supervision requires explaining things in discrete units with a methodological approach.

An individual whose dominant learning style is *abstract sequential* exists in a mental world and receives and produces information in a metaphysical and abstract manner. This individual responds to words and signs and mental pictures in constructing a concrete reality. Their thinking pattern is sequential and is likened to a two-dimensional geometry pattern. They view the world in a curvilinear fashion. The abstract sequential learning style is able to draw conclusions, predict the next step in the process, and become involved in the scope and sequence of the process. Supervision for this individual requires that they are active in the process and are allowed to draw their own conclusions during the supervision process. Although, initially they will require a more concrete approach to their professional practice it is a smooth and quick transition into seeing things from a synthesized perspective.

The *abstract random* learning style reflects and individual who is guided by feelings and emotions and lives in an abstract, non-physical world. Everything for this individual is "sensed." These are very imaginative people who view the world objectively. For them, the world is constantly moving and changing. Their order of thinking is non-linear and multidimensional. Events are viewed in a holistic manner. They do not view things as going from point A to point B. The individual with this learning style uses emotions and feelings as the baseline equation for all decision making. Supervision for this individual requires the supervisor to be extremely cognizant of this learning style. The abstract random individual will take anything the supervisor says to "heart." Their reaction to a supervisory experience will be emotional. Explaining events in concrete linear fashion will result in a negative experience for both the supervisor and the supervisee. The process of supervision requires approaching this individual in holistic and emotive manner.

The *concrete random* learning style consists of an individual who uses intuition in a concrete and physical world. This individual views the world in a three dimensional pattern. This individual sees the linear aspect of the world but also entertains the effects of outside variables that allow for deviation from a linear form. This learning style emphasizes intuition and instinct. A person with this dominant style is able to use his or her intuition and create order in a concrete and linear fashion. The process of supervision for this learning style is most successful when the supervisor sets the stage in a linear fashion and then allows the supervisee to make his own determinations based on instinct.

The supervisor's own dominant learning style will be a factor in the process of supervision. However, successful supervision relies on understanding the supervisee's learning style. It becomes the supervisor's responsibility to adapt his or her own dominant learning style in order to make the process of supervision successful for all supervisee's. The supervisor needs to match their reflective strategies to the learning style and the world-view of the supervisee.

The Synthesized Professional Supervision Model takes into account these various learning styles. By incorporating the learning styles of the supervisee into the process of supervision the transition from each stage takes on new meaning. The process then becomes individual and allows for the supervisee to grow and develop based on his or her own dominant style.

Developmental Paradigm

Developmental theory, although inherently dynamic, is often interpreted from a Newtonian paradigm. This results in viewing change over the life span in sequential stages where an individual is defined by the elements and characteristics at a particular point in time (age). It is important, therefore, to identify key principles that remain consistent. They are:

- People are not stages. Learning structures are slow to change and constructed in unique ways while being qualitatively different.

Positions, as termed by Perry (1970), provide a more fluid and *systemic* process in which to view growth. Developmental growth, consequently, occurs within the context of interacting members.

- The frame of development is more important than the specific elements.

- The inner logic (perception of meaning) is stressed as a structure of thought being expressed in a given behavior at a given moment (context).

- Developmental learning theories describe individual dynamics that aid in creating environments for presenting and processing information.

- Learning requires "facing up" to limits, uncertainties, and dissolution of beliefs to demand the undertaking for new decisions and forms of responsibility.

Two principles of developmental theory are especially applicable to adult education. The first is the term *scheme*. Piaget (1970) defined this as a pattern of stimuli and movements that activate as a whole. A scheme represents a "Gestalt with a history". It embodies past experience, generalizing and differentiating to varying contexts in varying ways. Scheme not only embodies what Bruner (1960) calls learning "structures" that aids in the transfer of principles and ideas to other areas, but nicely illustrates the concepts of perceptual patterning (Combs, 1954; Kelly, 1955) and the brain's function of learning by parallel processing wholes and parts simultaneously (Hart, 1983; Caine, 1990).

The second outlines the learning dynamics when addressing emotional states of *disequalibrium*. Piaget (1970) contends that information is either *assimilated* (generalized to the interacting context based on previous learning structures) or *accommodated* (changing a learning structure in response to a novel situation or stimuli). Consequently, an individual can either integrate the "novel" (Rotter, 1954) experience to previous learning schemes or change the quality of the scheme to "accommodate" the essence of the learning context. Selman (1980) identifies this learning process as a learner's drive for *equilibration*. He contends that students fit new experiences into previous schematas (assimilation) while also "discovering" new learning structures (accommodation) to retain stability. In this learning paradigm, the student is not a passive "blank slate", but an active learner able to rapidly process whole structures of knowledge and differentiate application to various contexts.

With his work on critical reflection, Mezirow (1991) affirms that individuals, in facing environmental demands, use their reflective systems. He asserts that within unfamiliar situations, individuals "create" new meaning schemes which make sense of *divergent* experiences. Kohlberg & Mayer (1972) illustrate this process in their progressive view of education. They advocate developing a learning environment that presents a graded series of experiences to "stimulate growth" for both assimilation and accommodation.

In a larger context, the dynamics associated with Piaget's (1970) concepts of scheme and disequalibrium provide a context for understanding learning and change within an interactive systems framework. General systems theory is based on the insight that a system as a whole is qualitatively different from the sum of the system's individual elements (Simon et al., 1985). Change in one part of a system (familial, educational, social, cultural, etc.) is followed by compensatory change in other parts of the system (Bowen, as cited in Schnarch, 1991). Reminiscent of Wertheimer's (1923) perceptual field theory, a systemic lens views the learner's (part) reality dependent upon the interactive quality and function of the system (whole). Wheatley (1994) highlights this point by emphasizing that the "part" is the whole. Any action of any part can manifest tranformative change to the whole.

Sheldrake (1981), in studying biological systems, postulates that when one member of a system assimilates a new learning structure (meaning or action), the system becomes "morphogenically" altered. Change, accordingly, occurs when the individual, within the context of learning, manages the "energy" (disequalibruim) to obtain new meaning or action that alters both the individual and his/her interacting system. From the context of supervision and instruction, therefore, providing opportunities for meaningful reflection on dissonant experiences enhances individual development as well as the development of others in which they interact. The reflective process is embedded in relational dynamics that can enhance supervision development as well as the professional growth necessary for improving the academic health of the schools in which they work. This professional growth, and the tasks related to each stage can be conceptualized through the following stages when conceptualizing professional development.

Self-centered stage

The premise of the self-centered stage is that the supervisee enters his/her new position with high levels of anxiety associated with performance and evaluation. This anxiety leads to patterns of dependency on the supervisor. During this stage the supervisee is uncertain and his/her self-confidence is shaky. Regardless of the pedagogical base the supervisee may have entered the job with, anxiety becomes heightened and the supervisee becomes dependent on the supervisor. In addition to the knowledge base required for the new position or the new school there is the issue of becoming familiar with the new organization, understanding the rules, policies, expectations, and becoming a member, of a new group of colleagues.

Supervisors need to determine what transitional stage the new supervisee is in. However, regardless of the stage the number one priority is to reduce anxiety and the level of dependency.

Client Centered Stage

During this stage the supervisee fluctuates between dependency and autonomy. The supervisee vacillates between being over-confident and being overwhelmed. As the supervisee becomes proficient confidence develops and the supervisee pulls back from dependency. However, if they make an error or encounter something new and different the supervisee will feel over-whelmed and exhibit dependent behaviors.

The supervisee hovers at the transitional line of his/her stage of development. As with each transitional shift an individual questions that part of his/her development in the client centered stage, the supervisee questions his/her confidence versus overwhelming fear of not succeeding

The common mistake made during this stage is the belief that the supervisee has moved from being dependent to being confident and independent. The belief that a supervisee moves from a low development to moderate development cognitive stage can be a misnomer. There is a half way step, the client-centered stage. The supervisee at times can generate solutions to problems and at times is unable to respond to problems. It is a back and forth movement from being dependent to being independent.

This stage is critical because the supervisee will either move toward the next stage or lose ground and go back to the self-centered stage. The role of the supervisor is crucial during this period. Supervision needs to be combination of collaborative and directive. The supervisor needs to encourage the independence by being a collaborative partner in the process of supervision. However, the moment that the supervisee displays dependency and a sense of being overwhelmed the supervisor needs to be directive by structuring a way for the supervisee to be independent!

Process centered and context centered

In the process centered stage the supervisee exhibits increased self-confidence and self-esteem and is able to look beyond the concrete aspects of the organization. In other words a teacher, for example, goes beyond a pedagogical base consisting of knowledge and skills and moves into a more thematic approach to instruction.

A student on the other hand begins to see him or herself as an important and worthwhile individual beyond what peers may be saying. That is not to say that peer influence diminishes, quite the contrary. However, the student is able to step beyond those parameters and develop self-confidence based on intrinsic value.

Both examples demonstrate the process- centered stage that supervisees evolve to provided supervision was effective in the previous stages. In the process -centered stage the supervisor needs to be supportive and encouraging. The supervisor needs to focus on the supervisees self-confidence, by fostering it in as many ways as possible.

This misconception also exists with students. The belief that a child moves rapidly from the self-centered stage to the context -centered stage within the first semester of school is erroneous. Again, the process is circular and children like adults jump back and forth between stages depending on whether needs have been met in previous stages or they are impacted by new experiences and/or peer influences.

With regard to adults, the SPSM has a foundation in adult development an area that has only been given attention in the past fifteen years. Levinson (1986) states that the goal of adult development is to create a life structure. This life structure is a pattern of life that consists of dreams, values, emotions, and the external aspects of work, family, relationships and religious life. Levinson has created a sequence of adult developmental periods that consist of eight stages.

Preadulthood occurs from conception till the age of twenty-two. Levinson places this as the zero stage, the basis for what is to follow. During this time people become biologically and psychologically separate from their parents or caretakers. Early adult transition is the first stage and occurs between the ages of seventeen and twenty-two. During this time people feel halfway out of their family. They have a tenuous sense of their own autonomy and feel that "real adulthood' is around the corner.

The second stage is entry life structure for adulthood. This occurs between the ages of twenty-two and twenty-eight. During this time people build on their adult life. They are established in a chosen lifestyle and pursue immediate goals without questioning whether they are following the right course. Age thirty transition is the third stage and occurs between the ages of twenty-eight and thirty- three. During this stage people often ask, "What is life about, now that I am doing what I am supposed to be doing?" "Is this the only way to be?" They often reassess both work and family patterns and may make changes.

The fourth stage occurs between the ages of thirty-three to forty and is referred to as the culminating life structure for early adulthood. During this time people make deeper commitments to work, family, and other important aspects of their lives, setting specific goals and timetables. Midlife transition is the fifth stage, which occurs between the ages of forty and forty-five. During this time people question every aspect of their lives with an increasing awareness that time is limited. The transition may be smooth or in a crisis proportion depending on personalities and past experiences.

Stage six is known as the age fifty transition and people have the opportunity to improve their life structure. Culminating life structure for middle adulthood occurs between fifty-five and sixty and is the seventh stage. This stage provides a framework for concluding middle adulthood. The final stage, late adult transition, which occurs after sixty, is the period that separates middle adulthood from late adulthood.

Another view of adult development comes from the work of Clausen (1986). Clausen states that there is no necessary sequence to the stages of adult development but rather people change in small ways throughout life. Some people undergo more transitions than others and some of Levinson's stages may overlap and occur in more circular patterns for people. Despite the differing theories surrounding adult development, one thing is clear, growth does not stop at the age of twenty-one. These stages or transitions impact on the level of supervisee development.

To date, most supervision models use as their pedagogical base developmental behavioral models and models of motivational theory. These have their place in supervision but to dismiss the unique aspects of adult development and the stages or transitions people go through perpetuates mediocrity within the field of supervision.

Pedagogy Paradigm

Each supervisee brings to his or her professional practice a pedagogical paradigm based on individual experience and knowledge. This individual experience and knowledge is the foundation for the practical theories that guide one's beliefs and professional actions. These practical theories are grounded in the cumulative life experiences and knowledge that the individual has gained. Practical theories are interrelated concepts, beliefs, and images that supervisees hold about their work. These practical theories guide the decision making process of the individual before, after, and during professional interaction.

McCutcheon (1995) states that practical theories are based largely on personal experiences. It is through these personal experiences that people construct meanings about the world. McCutcheon states that these experiences occur while growing up, going to school, working, traveling and interacting with people and the world. Supervisees create meanings through their various experiences about what is important to learn, about how others learn, about motivation, and about what is important to act upon and what is not. This is the culmination of one's practical theories.

Supervisees do not operate on the basis of a single practical theory but on the basis of a set of interrelated theories. Some aspects of one's practical theories are tacit, meaning the supervisee is unaware of them. It is through reflection and the process of supervision that these tacit theories move to the conscious level of the supervisee. These practical theories are also rational. They are intentional even though the supervisee may not be aware of the reasons for these intentional acts.

Acquiring knowledge, therefore, is the burden of the supervisor for matching their pedagogy to the needs of the supervisee and his/her learning style. This learner-centered ideology seeks not to change supervisees, but to design a learning environment and context where individuals can thrive, reason, and change themselves. It is clear that learning environments must be designed not to instruct, but to influence: to stimulate the natural processes of learning and change. This is represented in the following active principles of pedagogy.

Learning is Reflective

"...the knowledge of knowledge compels" (Maturana, 1987, p.245)

Schon (1987) defines reflection as *knowing-in-action*, and explains, "When the practitioner reflects-in-action in a case he perceives as unique, paying attention to phenomena and surfacing his intuitive understanding of them, his experimenting is a once exploratory, move testing, and hypothesis testing. The three functions are fulfilled by the very same actions". (p.72). Instruction, therefore, is encouraged to reflect in the moment of action (teaching) in the same way students are invited to reflect on their learning. To achieve this, however, practitioners are confronted with a paradox rooted in traditional linear models advocating prescribed and sequential practices. As Schon (1987) eloquently puts it, "In order to gain that sense of competence, control, and confidence that characterize professionals, students of professional practice must first give it up" (p. 72).

This paradox of instruction and learning, calling for a shift to more complex levels of cognitive processing, is consistent with Bertrand Russel's (1910) theory of *logical types*. He indicates that in order to establish a class, a shift is needed to understand a collection of objects (i.e. a group of chairs to the concept of furniture). To focus on the analysis of each part is to maintain a homeostatic and repetitious cycle of stagnated growth maintained by embedded beliefs. Schnarch (1991) identifies this transformation in writing, "Inherent paradox often surfaces at the interface between the drive for change and growth, and the drive for stability and homeostasis" (p. 480).

Addressing this paradox and encouraging others to shift to a higher order of conceptual processing lies in reflective practice. Rather than focus on problem solving of content, meaningful learning occurs through self-examination of assumptions, patterns of interactions, and the operating premises of action. This emphasis on critical reflection can lead to transformational learning exhibited through reflective action consistent with a change in premise. Additionally, Tessmer (1993) states that concepts are more than "classification rules" and that instructional design needs to foster proper schema-like connections with prior knowledge and encourage inference to productive action and change. He proposes the use of teaching with *analogies, concept mapping* and structuring to meaningful contexts, and the use of *inference practice*. By advocating a broader stance in addressing conceptual education, "reflective practice" to move beyond the collection of rules to shifting schemes of belief.

Learning is Complex and Authentic

"One is unable to notice something because it is always before one's eyes" (Staten, 1984, p.76)

Many perspectives represent learning. The aim of a pedagogical framework for supervisors and supervisees is to bring forth worlds that accommodate or reflect the views of others (Knuth, 1993). The utilization of discourse, where the focus is on understanding justifications rather than determining truth promotes the presentation of multiple points of view, free from coercion, that provide opportunities for critical reflection. It is the awareness of the "larger context" and encourages instruction that emphasizes cultural, social, gender, and historical origins of student constructs. What is effective in one context, with one learner or group of learners, or for one purpose may be severely dysfunctional in another context, with different people, or for another purpose (Brookfield, 1990).

Hart (1983) argued that the complexity of learning involves 1) promoting positive student *expectation*, 2) developing *ambiance* where learning is free from threat, 3) identifying *mastery* as the learning goal, and 4) creating learning experiences that focus on the *active participation* of learning patterns for the natural transfer of learning. Caine (1990) mirrors this approach with complex interactive experiences he calls *immersion*. Creating a learning setting for relaxed alertness, instruction is designed to engage the entire self of the learner and provide meaningful participation through reflection, contemplation, creative elaboration, combination processes and action designed around self reorganization. Appelton (1990) outlines instructional interventions consistent with brain theory concepts. They are:

- Identify preconceptions
- Provide a new encounter
- Link ideas to learning patterns
- Provide corrective feedback
- Avoid false assumptions from the learners
- Prevent opting out
- Help towards accommodation
- Applying new ideas
- Diagnosis and remediation

Knowledge is Action

"*Every act of knowing brings forth a world...[so] all doing is knowing and all knowing is doing*" (Maturana, 1987, p. 26)

Kolb's (1984) experiential learning theory presents a framework helpful consistent with reflective supervision and instruction for with regard to academic health. He suggests that learning occurs as individuals move through a cycle of concrete experience, reflective observation, abstract conceptualization, and active experimentation. Involving all four modes will be sensitive to various learning styles while challenging them to develop other ways of learning as well. His theory emphasizes the dialectical nature of human interactions in experience within a four stage cyclical model. The model begins with a concrete experience on which a person observed and reflects, forms generalizations, goes on to test implications in new situations, and then repeats the cycle. Kolb states that the immediate concrete experience is the basis for observation and reflection. An individual uses these observation to build an idea, generalization, or a theory from which new implications can be made. These new implications serve as a guide in creating new experiences.

The process of supervision requires the supervisors understanding of the supervisee's pedagogy. A supervisees pedagogy, or practical theory, forms the basis for reasoning. This pedagogy guides the supervisee's actions during professional practice. Without a complete understanding of the supervisee's pedagogy the process of supervision will not serve to develop the supervisee to his or her fullest potential. This pedagogical paradigm will be elaborated on later.

Cultural Paradigm

Multicultural education has been on the forefront of American education for some time. Teachers are constantly reminded of the need to celebrate diversity within the classrooms and the importance of teaching children to accept people who are different from them. Advocates of multicultural education value the attributes of cultural, ethnic, and racial diversity, as well as human rights, social justice, equitable distribution of power, and equal opportunity. However understanding and implementing multicultural education in school can be quite distinct processes. Educators and school leaders to identify what school practices are being undertaken in the name of multicultural education and the differences these practices make to the academic health of their students. Is "meaningful

Multiculturalism" a meaning-filled expression, or is it only an empty banality that, like so many slogans, only blurs and confused good intentions?

All supervision, counseling, and educational contacts have cultural, racial-ethnic aspects which shape core assumptions, attitudes, and values of the persons involved and which may enhance or impede professional and student effectiveness. The supervisor and counselor without thought often accept however, a majority of cultural patterns present in the process of leadership, counseling, and instruction. The supervisors role is to promote supervisee growth by challenging cultural assumptions, encouraging emotional expression, and validating conflict of attitudes and values. In other words, faculty, administrators, and parents need to deliberately confront what Bernard and Goodyear (1992) entitled the "Myth of Sameness" present in all educational interactions. With an awareness for reflective learning, early discussion of supervisor and supervisee racial-ethnic backgrounds and expectations about supervision may help establish a base for the development of trust so important in creating and maintaining academic health in schools.

This is supported in a study by Ladany, Brittan-Powell, and Pannu (1997) who contend that supervisors who have a higher racial consciousness are able to empathize with supervisees who are at lower levels of racial consciousness and who exhibit sensitivity to the supervisee's racial identity status. This finding implies that supervisees are able to become more multiculturally competent when given the opportunity, and that supervisors can play a large role in influencing supervisee development. Furthermore, it challenges schools and school leaders/supervisors to obtain and provide training in promoting racial identity development.

Even within our own day to day living experiences we are constantly reminded of the fact that America is a great "melting pot." However, in the process of supervision the respect and understanding for diversity is something that falls by the wayside.

Sorting through the research on supervision reveals a lack of responsiveness to the cultural paradigm of the supervisee. The closest any research comes to culture is found in the work of Bowers and Flinders (1990, 1991). Bowers and Flinders argue for a culturally responsive supervision model. They argue that supervision needs to move away from the view that events that occur are the outcomes of rationally motivated actions of the supervisees and their subordinates. They propose that understanding the events that a supervisor observes is a manifestation of the cultural ecology of the environment (i.e. classrooms).

The work of Bowers and Flinders focuses on teaching, teachers and classrooms. From their perspective teachers and supervisors need to become sensitive and responsive to the fact that a classroom is embedded in a social and cultural context. Bowers and Flinders maintain that the social issues of drug abuse, poverty, gender, racial discrimination, religious differences, and environmental concerns all influence events in the classroom. They state that the perceptions and behavior patterns of students, teachers, and supervisors are culturally determined. They believe that supervisors need to sensitize teachers to these issues. Bowers and Flinders state that the recognition of the social and cultural embeddedness of classroom events should guide the teacher's actions, as well as the supervisor's observations, and the relationship between the supervisor and the teacher.

Bowers and Flinders present a compelling position for the need for teachers and supervisor's to be aware of the cultural embeddedness within the classroom. However, their work needs to be taken to an earlier step, the cultural embeddedness of the supervisee.

The Synthesized Professional Supervision Model proposes that supervisors need to be aware of the cultural paradigm of the supervisee. The supervisee comes to an organization with embedded beliefs. These beliefs are fostered by the individual's race, gender, and religion. In addition, the social issues of addiction, poverty, discrimination, and environmental concerns affect the supervisee's professional practice. Therefore, the process of supervision cannot negate the cultural paradigm.

A supervisor needs to be aware of the supervisee's gender, race, and religious beliefs. The manner in which the supervisee conducts him or herself is guided by the above mentioned factors. It is erroneous for a supervisor to believe that he or she can supervise all supervisee's the same. The supervisee's cultural paradigm is embedded in his or her reaction to the process of supervision and improvement of professional practice. Understanding each supervisee's cultural paradigm will enable the supervisor to form a more trusting relationship with the supervisee. It will enable the supervisor to assist the supervisee in the various phases of supervision in a meaningful way. Recognizing each supervisee's cultural paradigm enables the supervisor to individualize the process of supervision for each supervisee. This leads to a process of supervision that is successful with every aspect of professional practice and growth.

Conclusion

Research has indicated that there are similarities among the models of supervision in educational leadership and counseling. These models when combined offer the potential of a problem solving process hinged on the professional growth of the practitioner (Knoff, 1988). However, little if any work has been done to combine these models. What has not emerged is a new model of supervision that crosses the disciplines of education and counseling for assisting educators to address the academic health of their students and relational atmosphere in their schools, until now. The Synthesized Professional Supervision Model addresses these gaps and proposes a comprehensive framework for understanding not only professional growth but also strategies that supervisors can use to directly influence the quality and depth of the supervisee development. This new model crosses disciplines in an effective, in depth and holistic manner.

In addressing traditional linear education and supervision, the challenge rests with staying present in the process and not preoccupied with the product. John Kabat-Zinn (1995) illustrates this nicely when he writes, "If we hope to go anywhere or develop ourselves in any way, we can only step from where we are standing. If we don't really know where we are standing---a knowing that comes directly from the cultivation of mindfulness---we may only go in circles, for all our efforts and expectations.....So (in practice), the best way to get somewhere is to let go of trying to get anywhere at all" (p.16). The following chapter attempts to provide specific suggestions and scenarios for the application of this supervision model "mindful" of school context. Furthermore, recommendations for how the use of this model can increase the academic health of schools while decreasing unhealthy school environments will be reviewed. Lastly, a series of reflective questions will guide the reader for assessing the academic health of their school or school district while providing benchmarks for areas of growth.

Chapter 5

Creating Academically Healthy Schools with the SPSM

As with any new idea or program the question automatically becomes, how do I do this? Tell me the way to carry out this new idea or program. There is no "cookie cutter" recipe to implementing the Synthesized Professional Supervision Model in the creation of academically healthy schools. There can't be. Each school is different with a different climate and culture. Just on a basic level there are elementary, middle or junior high, and high schools. There are urban, suburban, and rural areas. There is the northeast, mid east, southeast, mid west, southwest and western regions. All of these aspects lead to different populations of students, faculty, staff, parents and community members. However, there are basic key concepts that should be learned and adopted in order to create an academically healthy school.

First we must begin with the relationship of the school leader to his/her school and the relationship between the school leader and school counselor, an instrumental person in the implementation of this model. Sergiovanni (1998) states that leaders have failed in schools because leadership is viewed as a behavior rather than an action and having to do with persons rather than ideas.

Leadership is not a position but a relationship. Research indicates that school leadership has failed because of the managerial mystique. There is a mistaken belief that leadership is linked to management and the correct way to do things. School leaders have lost sight and have forgotten that leadership is about purpose and not procedures. The intent of the SPSM is to establish a trusting relational context that assists others in "making sense" of dissonant and uncertain professional/learning experiences. This requires a commitment. A commitment to the time and accessibility needed to transform anxiety and uncertainty to meaningful developmental change with administrators, faculty, and students.

This investment of time is the only way to ensure an exponential return in the academic health of students throughout their educational tenure. Districts can not lose sight of long-term goals in pursuit of short-term rewards. To expect teens to heed words for nonviolence when a context of trust has not been established is an educational practice that only does not work, but makes little sense to what we know about change. The essence of the SPSM is the willingness for school leaders to be assessable to faculty and faculty to be assessable to students while the complexities for long-term change are addressed.

The long history of educational systems to prioritize the product over the person, the test scores over the process of learning and hierarchical power structures over collaborative decision making will make the implementation of SPSM difficult and seemingly ambiguous. However, for the many reasons to maintain the status quo educational interactions and focus, there is only one needed to change: violence. If we expect the educational system to produce, as Jefferson proported, good citizens school leaders need first to demonstrate their citizenship to students...

Sergiovanni (1998) points out that the heart of leadership has to do with what a person believes, values, and is committed to. It is shaped by the heart and has to do with reflection, which in turn leads to actions and behaviors. These values and beliefs are influenced by the interpersonal relationship that a leader has with teachers and staff. Leadership involves the leaders understanding the values and beliefs of teachers and staff. Sergiovannis' move toward moral leadership is timely within a school society that is filled with potential violence.

It merits repeating, leadership is a relationship. Leaders are not meant to be superhuman, all knowing and all seeing. It is an art, an encounter. It is something that is experienced in an interaction with another. It is a relationship that is based on the mutual needs and interests between the leader and his/he constituents. In order to establish this relationship, leaders must be honest, forward looking, inspiring, and competent. They need to be consistent and yet change over time, have global and local expectations (Kouzes & Posner, 1993).

Sergiovanni (1998) proposed that we need to develop a sense of moral authority. This moral authority takes its form in obligations and duties that are derived from widely shared values, ideas, and ideals. Everyone is responding to shared commitments and interdependence. Moral authority is the obligations and duties that are derived from widely shared professional and community values, ideas and ideals that become the center stage of schools.

Schools need to move toward creating learning communities that focus on the relationships among students, teachers, staff, parents, administrators and the larger community. It needs to hold shared values, beliefs, and commitments that bond each person to the community. In so doing leaders lead their school toward the model of being academically healthy.

Leaders need to establish relationships that allow teachers to move beyond teaching as knowledge and move toward the practical problems of everyday living that children must face. A code of ethics needs to be brought back into the school. This code of ethics should be the heart of the leadership relationship. In addition the leadership relationship must promote a firm belief in communication that encompasses the learning community. Creating academically healthy schools requires creating healthy relationships as a foundation.

Once the relationships have been established and formed then everyone in the school needs to be instructed regarding utilization of the model. It is key that each school decides as an individual community the best method for implementing the model based on their individual needs. However, there are basic premises that should be adopted as part of the implementation.

Everyone has to recognize that each member of the school community goes through the various stages described under the fist two frames of the model; supervisory reflective cycle and supervisee stage of professional development. There has to be an understanding that the stages of child and adult development will determine the cycle each individual is in. Appropriate supervision ensues based on identification of the stage that the child, adolescent, or adult is in. The following is a description of how the SPSM can be utilized in assessing supervisees and students while providing interventions that match to their unique worldviews and learning needs. Themes of developmental growth through a reflective cycle of interaction will also be presented as well as examples of application with faculty and students.

Assessment

Within the supervisory relationship the supervisor needs to assess the supervisee/student in accordance to the framework of the SPSM. Identifying the developmental level of the supervisee as well as the phase of the supervisory relationship can assist as supervisors in matching reflective interventions to assist in the concurrent growth of both. Further understanding of the supervisee's learning style as well as the pedagogical and cultural worldview as discussed in Chapter 4 will provide additional insights. This increased understanding of the supervisee not provides valuable for the level and intent of the of supervisory interventions and focus, but continues to increased the safety and trust needed to encourage supervisees/student for initiating graduated risk taking experiences.

Themes for Supervisory Matching Interventions

As dissonant experiences are transformed into meaningful schemas and corresponding counseling skills, the supervisee develops in concert with the progression of the on-site supervision relationship. This model of dynamic interchange illustrates the concurrent development of both supervisees and the supervision relationship leading to increased professional and educational independence of practitioners and students (see figure 6). It is through the use of reflective learning strategies that supervisors and educators can assist in this developmental growth in reference to their learning style as well as their level pedagogical intent and cultural understanding. A supervisory reflective framework can be integrated to each stage of developmental growth, which encourages supervisees/students to examine their assumptions and internationalities while exploring new roles for increased risk taking within the professional and/or learning environment. The following are additional reflective experiences that can promote reflective understanding:

Journaling

A writing out of confusions, frustrations, questions, intentions, hypotheses, and assumptions pertaining to a peer, client, student, instructional or counseling event.

Reflective Discussion

Reviewing experiences either with the supervisor or peers in terms of what happened and what is being learned. A planned discussion of culture and the culture of practice as well as the exploration of supervisee/supervisor cultural backgrounds is recommended

Retrospection

Drawing together materials (case notes, reflective pad, literature, etc.) linking to the articulation of those values, beliefs, and concepts that guide professional practice and learning.

Action Research

This may involve a review of the literature and application of the relevant findings to the practice and tasks of teaching and/or counseling as well as a study of their own practice.

Co-therapy and Collaborative Professional Projects

Initiating and engaging in a collaborative effort, in an instructional, administrative, and/or counseling setting or in a community based project, with a peer for a sharing of ideas, energy, and action.

Taping of instructional/counseling/supervision sessions

Self- assessment is an active use of reviewing and reflecting on professional practice. Self and peer review of instructional, counseling, and/or supervision sessions can assist with becoming more deliberate with one's strengths as well as identifying goals for improvement.

Modeling

Identifying advanced practitioners willing to provide shadowing opportunities. Observing the style and intent of other professionals can initiate a shift in context necessary to stimulate continued growth and reflection.

By assisting practitioners and students in "making sense" of dissonant educational experiences academic health of schools can be. Understanding that growth is reciprocal and in concert with others is the cornerstone of reflective learning. It also provides a context for matching this reflective process to the learning style and developmental preferences of the supevisee/student.

Dependence to Autonomy

New professionals and students enter the school experience emotionally and cognitively overwhelmed while dependent on the supervisor/teacher for providing structured guidance and encouragement in orienting to the school context. Through continued exposure to the school context and related supervisory/instructional dynamics, the supervisees/students anxieties lessen; he/she becomes more independent in conceptualizing their learning process and determining areas of both professional and personal growth. Supervision needs to provide a supportive and reassuring context for instruction for assisting with orientating to the school context while facilitating a trusting supervisory relationship for promoting advanced conceptual development. The development of greater conceptual complexity of practitioners and student provide a foundation for the final phase of supervision development focused on increasing the autonomy of trainees/students in both their clinical self assessment and practice. The dimensions of supervisee experience, therefore, articulate processes central to their becoming independent school counseling professionals.

High School Example

For example, a freshman in high school is going to be at the first stage of both of these frames. The student is going to be anxious with a perceived sense of inadequacy and will demonstrate high levels of anxiety associated with performance in the academic and social arena. These students need more supervision than the student who is a senior in high school. The school would do well to run group meetings throughout the year for all students. These groups should meet weekly if possible and should be spearheaded by the counselors in conjunction with teachers. All should be communicated to the school leader. The purpose is to guide the students to the next level of development under these frames and to be able to denote any problems or difficulties, academically and/or socially, immediately. This process gives the school an in-depth understanding of each freshman that will carry itself through the course of the students' high school career.

If you follow the model than the "supervisor", in this example, the school counselor and teachers are non-judgmental, supportive, and validating. They work toward making the student independent and secure in his or her abilities. The intent is to move the student to the higher levels within the supervisee stage of development. It is key to note that many students will vacillate between the stages based on the factors that influence their lives. These factors are established in the third frame, supervisee paradigms influencing practice. The students' cultural background, learning style, reflective style, and pedagogical base all impact on the overall development. Academically healthy schools are predicated on the notion that familial, cultural, and emotional aspects all influence the health of a school.

These factors can be discovered through weekly meetings or another method that a school may find more effective. Maybe, in-depth surveys can be completed by the student, or the Gregoric given in order to establish the students learning style, or any other similar inventory. The point is that it is critical that the student be viewed as a whole person and that all of these aspects be investigated and understood so that the student may move through the various stages in a healthy manner. It allows for potential problems to be "nipped in the bud." However, we recognize that nothing is absolute and students with needs could still be missed. Yet, the likelihood of that happening is greatly reduced with this model.

The final frame, phases of supervision, flows naturally once the first three frames have been simultaneously implemented. Staying with our example, freshmen are going to experience an adjustment period to such a model, there will be a level of discomfort until they realize that the experience is positive and they establish trust in between and among themselves and the staff. Eventually the suggested meetings will move to a level of dialogue among the students that leads to self-autonomy and the ability to self-assess one's own situation.

Elementary School Example

As you comprehend this concept it becomes clear that this model encompasses every aspect of an individuals development. The above example may make it easy to understand and palatable when discussing a high school student. What about an elementary school student? How does it work? Basically with the same premise but geared toward the developmental stage of a younger child. However, utilization of this model must begin in the elementary schools, this is critical.

A kindergarten child, for example, enters school with a high sense of anxiety and fears of inadequacy. The anxiety and fears are tied to a new experience as well as the separation from mom and dad. In some cases, it is also separation from younger siblings, or increased anxiety based on performance of older siblings. The child becomes dependent on the kindergarten teacher. In addition, the child's cultural background, family history, learning style, ability to reflect on the situation and pedagogy which is based on the pre-operational levels of Piaget impact on the process of moving toward the higher level of autonomy. The child also has to adjust to a new climate, the school climate.

Schools have an exceptional opportunity in implementing this model from the very beginning. By taking extensive histories prior to entering kindergarten and through observations of the classroom teacher, support teachers, and specialists, such as counselors a complete and whole picture of each child will develop. Kindergarten is the grade where team meetings should be held quarterly to discuss each child. Parents should be involved so that the familial aspects of an academically healthy school are being met. A profile of each child should be developed that will follow the student from grade to grade. This is synthesized supervision. This allows for a continual process of fostering the growth of each child through each stage and being able to re-circle when the child goes back to the initial stages. Children will reach the levels of autonomy but easily move back to the first level of perceived doubt and anxiety when some significant change occurs in their lives. This change can be physical, family related (such as divorce, death, illness or the birth of a new child), it can be social, or related to moving from elementary to middle to high school. It is guaranteed that children like adults will continually cycle through this model. It is part of human development!

Faculty Example

School leaders in adopting the synthesized professional supervision model must first recognize that supervision is not evaluation. They are not synonymous.

Supervision is about the growth and development of people. Therefore, supervision of faculty is for each member's self-growth, self-esteem, and self-efficacy. However, the models of supervision as discussed in chapter three only focuses on the growth and development of the teacher in terms of teacher performance as it relates to student achievement. Growth and development of teacher performance is critical and directly related to student achievement. Yet it is a narrow focus. In order for a teacher to improve professionally, supervision must include the aspects of culture, reflectivity, learning style, and pedagogy. This allows for a synthesized form of supervision.

As indicated in chapter three there are many models of supervision, each with its own merits, yet each lacking something another model has. Clinical supervision focuses very distinctly on a circular process that allows for improving teacher performance with the effect of improving student achievement. Instructional supervision models also focus on teacher performance and is a reconceptualized version of clinical supervision that allows for more fluctuation and creativity.

Both of these models appear to lack attention to adult development. The developmental supervision model gives attention to adult development using as its pedagogical base, Maslow's theory of motivation. Developmental supervision models give tremendous attention to adult cognitive development, conceptual development, moral development and ego development with the premise that attention to these facets will lead to improved teacher performance. Yet, the individuals' pedagogical beliefs are not taken into account with this model. Moral supervision theories are based on the need to first understand the values and beliefs of teachers that lead to shared beliefs, values, and commitments. Again, the belief is that focusing on these facets leads to better teacher performance that will benefit students. The reality is that all of these models need to be integrated along with counseling theories for an effective method of supervision that provides for an academically healthy environment for faculty and staff.

The synthesized professional supervision model is as easily adapted for faculty as it is for students. The critical point to be made is that the entire school community is operating from this model. This consistency and holistic approach allows for the solid development of an academically healthy environment. School leaders need to refocuses, not be concerned with yearly evaluations, not concerned with only one facet of supervision but be concerned with all aspects of synthesized supervision for each of their staff members.

A school leader first needs to do an analysis of what stage of development each faculty member is at. In other words a novice teacher, one who has been a teacher for less than three years, is at the first level of each frame of the SPSM. With this knowledge a school leader should be able to recognize that a novice teacher is going to feel anxious and have a perceived sense of inadequacy. The teacher is going to be dependent on other teachers and the administrator for support. The novice teacher should be dependent, however our schools are set up so that the expectation for a novice teacher is that they are functioning at the highest level of the SPSM, with complete autonomy and self-assessment. No wonder the attrition rate in the teaching profession is so high. No wonder teachers cannot recognize troubled children like those at Columbine High.

A teacher who is not a novice is generally experienced. The level of autonomy is dependent on the number years the teacher has been in the profession. Of course it should be recognized that a teacher who has changed grade levels or is new to the district and experienced will move back to the initial stages but moves through the stages again very quickly. Teachers that are marginal or passive regarding their teaching may be in this position because supervision until this time has been poor.

A school leader would do well to begin the school year by determining each teachers learning style, simply done with an inventory at a faculty meeting.

Of course the faculty must first be made aware of the SPSM and be invested in creating an academically healthy school. Once the leader has a clear understanding of each teacher's learning style, through open discussion, the school leader can come to a complete understanding of each teachers' pedagogical beliefs, cultural and familial influences and reflectivity style. The time invested in doing this is worthwhile. This is the same method that teachers and counselors will be using with students. It is a school wide supervision model.

In addition a school leader should have a clear understanding of the adult development stages of people like Levinson as described in Chapter 3. A persons' level of adult development will also impact on their position in the SPSM. It is paramount that there be a comprehensive picture of each faculty member similar to the comprehensive picture of each student.

Once the school leader has this understanding than supervision becomes complete, meaningful, and promotes the entire growth of the faculty member. This in turn influences the student on every level not just in terms of academic achievement. If the leader understands each faculty member then supervision flows based on the level the teacher is at. So a novice teacher is obviously going to need more encouragement and support. An experienced teacher is going to be autonomous and self-assessing. Teaching style will be impacted by the teachers learning style, pedagogical beliefs, reflective practices, cultural, and familial influences. If a school leader understands this then the ability to assist the teacher in self-growth that impacts on the overall school community is easy. It is the initial investment that takes time but once the leader invests this time while the teachers and counselors are investing their time with understanding the students then the ongoing utilization of the model becomes easy. Remember we are not talking about evaluations we are talking about supervision, a model for creating academically healthy schools.

Children and adolescents are struggling with identifying themselves and others. Adults even struggle with their own identification. Schools need to promote self-esteem and self-efficacy within an academic environment. In order to do this, schools need to recognize the facets that create an academically healthy school; the emotional, familial, cultural, academic and administrative processes. Aggression and violence in our schools will only continue to fester and grow unless we begin a model of supervision that is holistic and encompasses every facet of human development. In adopting such a model, the creation of academically healthy schools will occur, and the microcosm of schools can move to eradicating acts of aggression and violence that lead to the millions of deaths of children every day. Schools once again can become whole and healthy with each member being intertwined in a model of supervision that promotes the growth, self-esteem, and self-efficacy of each individual. Leaders need this model so they can fully understand each faculty member and promote their development. This in turn allows for the faculty to use this model in understanding students because they are being understood. Students then see that everyone is engaged in this process and they are able to utilize the model and understand one another. It becomes a circular process that allows for creating an environment that foster the healthy microcosm of schools based on the healthy aspects of society at large.

It is the influence of the person over the performance; it is care toward empowerment, not persuasion. We are all bound by similar struggles. Are we less frustrated in not being able to meet professional demands or performance? Are students less saddened by these same facets? Is there an absence of passion when united by a common vision and theme when making an impact in the world around us? We think not.

Chapter 6

Metaphorically Speaking

Creating academically healthy schools via the Synthesized Professional Supervision Model can be visualized as the "mother ocean". Like a lot of ocean-fronts we build structures too close to the water where the forces of nature erode the foundation of what is built. Despite continued rebuilding efforts, the structure continues to erode. We blame "mother ocean", blind to the relationship we establish with the ocean.

Similarly with schools we built a structure over a hundred years ago founded on a factory model of "producing" students managed with a Theory X philosophy. It was a model weak in relationship to schools and society at large. When that model eroded we switched to a more humanistic approach evoking creativity and empowerment. As with ocean front properties another storm arrived and we went back to basics and standardization. Now learning and effective teaching is measured by state mandates and test scores. It is still ineffective. The result has been the storm of all storms, violence in schools. So we are looking to rebuild; again. What a mistake! Simply put, it is the relationship with our communities at large that need to be forged. The relationship with society that needs to be built. It is not the foundation, the mortar and the bricks. It is the poor relationship we have established with "mother ocean."

Part of the problem is that we think in a linear fashion. A causes B that causes C. There is no thought to the fact that B causes A! This linear thinking is limiting. As Peter Senge (1990) points out when we think in linear ways we perceive the world as linear. We need to restructure our thinking and think in terms of systems and circles instead of straight lines. So it is with schools. If we do A then B will happen. If we raise standards then everyone will achieve. If we make teachers accountable by evaluating them then we can raise the quality of teaching. If we test children with standardized tests then we will know what they are learning. Currently, if we police schools, use metal detectors and take a no tolerance policy violence will end.

However, all of these linear thoughts have failed and are failing. We need fluid thinking. We need to understand that academics are more than content areas. We need to understand that supervision is not evaluation. We need to understand that supervision extends to every member of the school community. To develop a systems relationship requires us to create academically healthy schools premised on a fluid supervision model.

Visualizing the synthesized professional supervision model takes us back to the image of "mother ocean." The ocean rolls into the land in circular motions with soft waves or fierce waves. At times the ocean rolls upon the sand in a gentle comforting motion and at other times it hits hard. The waves of the ocean are sometimes calm and comforting and at times crash upon the rocks with sternness. The ocean itself is placid one day and irritated the next. In addition, the ocean washes many things upon the sand: shells, rocks, seaweed, to name a few. As one walks along the beach you can pick up and touch each of these items and place them back or pick them up and string them together to create a unified picture of what the ocean has to offer.

So it is with supervision. It is a fluid system not a linear one. At times it is calm and other times it is difficult and rough. People move from one stage of development to another and back again in a circular motion depending on experiences, knowledge, culture, family values and beliefs. In schools, supervision is a fluid process that includes administrators, staff, and students. It is not about accountability. It is about creating academically healthy environments founded on trust and care for all within the school community. Until we understand that we need to create a relationship with communities and society, until we understand that A does not necessarily cause B, until we start thinking in a fluid manner we will perpetuate results similar to the eroded structures on ocean fronts.

School violence is not solved solely by policing or zero tolerance policies. Again it is not a linear solution, it requires a fluid approach. As usual we have become reactionary to school violence to the extreme point of suspending a kindergarten child for having a water pistol. We need to be proactive and understand the complexities of human relations. The Synthesized Professional Supervision model is complex, but so are the problems being witnessed in schools today. The SPSM in its complexity addresses the multifaceted dynamics of human relationships. In addressing school violence the SPSM reminds us that school violence is not about violence but about kids and that has to do with all of us involved with them. The SPSM is as complex as the universe yet in its complexity lies a very simple answer: understand the dynamics of all, supervise based on these dynamics and academically healthy schools that go beyond mere academic content will occur. As for school violence it will dissipate like the unexpected storm once we deal with the underlying current.

Focus Questions

How academically healthy is your school? The following questions are to be used as a starting point in for both personal reflection as well as dialogue with school leaders and faculty.

- ❑ Do students exhibit behaviors that indicate positive attitudes and enthusiasm towards teachers, peers, family, and academic pursuits? If so, how do you monitor each student? If not what forms of assessment and intervention could you develop?

- ❑ Does all staff exhibit behaviors that indicate positive attitudes and enthusiasm toward students, peers, parents, and professional pursuits. If so, how do you foster the adult development of each staff member? If not what could you do to foster this development?

□ Are you aware of your own level of professional development and goals for continued growth as a person and practitioner? Have you discussed these with your supervisor? Why or why not?

□ How would you rate the level of trust between faculty; between students; and between parents with regard to the learning process of students?

□ Do you know who the children of trauma are in your school? If so, how are relationships being established in your school to reach out to them?

□ What is being modeled in your school about passionate learning and reflective knowledge?

□ Does your school utilize a fluid model of supervision for all? If not is your school willingly to take the necessary steps to create such a model?

□ How will the vision of the school need to shift in order to have a fluid model of supervision and create academically healthy schools?

□ What are the steps of change your school will need to take in order to become academically healthy?

□ How will the structure and the roles of your school shift in developing a fluid model of supervision for creating academically healthy schools?

□ Finally, how committed are you and your school organization to a major mind shift for the future of public education?

References

Acheson, K.A. & Gall, M.D. (1997). <u>Techniques in the clinical</u> <u>supervision of teachers.</u> (4th ed.). NY: Longman

Appleton, K. (1994). Using learning theory to guide reflection in the practicum. <u>Educational Resource Information Service</u>.

Argyris, C. (1957). <u>Personality and organization</u>. Harper and Row: NY

Bateson, G., Jackson, D., Haley, J., & Weakland, J. (1956). Toward a theory of schizophrenia. <u>Behavioral Science, 1</u>, 251-264.

Bernard, J. M., & Goodyear, R. K. (1992). <u>Fundamentals of clinical</u> <u>supervision</u>. Boston: Allyn and Bacon.

Berreth, D. & Berman, S. (May, 1997). "The Moral Dimensions of Schools,' <u>Educational Leadership</u>, 54, 8, pp.24-27.

Blumstein, A. (December,1995). "Youth, violence, guns and illicit drug markets," <u>National Institute of Justice Research Preview.</u>

Borders, L. D. (1989). A pragmatic agenda for developmental supervision research. <u>Counselor Education and Supervision, 29</u>, 16-24.

Borders, L. D. (1989). A pragmatic agenda for developmental supervision research. <u>Counselor Education and Supervision, 29</u>, 16-24.

Borders, L. D. (1989). Developmental cognitions of first practicum supervisees. <u>Journal of Counseling Psychology, 36</u>(2), 163-169.

Borders, L. D. (1989). Developmental cognitions of first practicum supervisees. <u>Journal of Counseling Psychology, 36</u>(2), 163-169.

Bowen, M. (1966). The use of family theory in clinical practice. <u>Comprehensive Psychiatry, 7</u>, 345-374.

Bowers, C.A. & Flinders, D.J. (1990). <u>Responsive teaching: An ecolgogical</u> <u>approach to</u>

Bowers, C.A. & Flinders, D.J. (1991). <u>Culturally responsive teaching and</u> <u>supervsion: A handbook for staff development</u>. NY: Teachers College Press.

Brookfield, S. D. (1987). <u>Developing critical thinkers</u>. San Francisco: Jossey-Bass Publishers Inc.

Bruner, J. (1960). <u>The process of education</u>. New York: Vintage Books: A division of Random House.

Burns, J. M. (1978). <u>Leadership.</u> NY: Harper and Row.

Caine, N. R., & Caine G. (1994). <u>Making connections: Teaching and the human brain</u>. Menlo Park, California.: Addison-Wesley,.

Callahan, R. (1962). <u>Education and the cult of efficiency.</u> Chicago, IL: University of Chicago Press.

Canada, G. (1995). <u>Fist, stick, knife, gun</u>. Boston: Beacon Press. <u>Classoom patems of language, culture and thought</u>. NY: Teachers College Press.

Clausen, J. (1986). "Early adult choices and the life course," Paper presented the 81st annual meeting of the American Sociological Association.

Combs, A. W. (1954). Counseling as a learning process. <u>Journal of Clinical Psychology, 1</u>, 31-36.

Davies, M. (1976). Systems theory and social work. In J. P. Beshon, G. (Ed.), <u>Systems Behavior</u> (2nd ed.,). New York: Harper & Row.

Dewey, J. (1938). <u>Experience and education</u>. New York: Macmillan.

Dohrn, B. (Oct. 1997). "Youth violence: False fears and hard truths." <u>Educational Leadership</u>, 55,2, pp.45-47

Dykeman, C., Daehlin, W., Doyle, S., & Flamer, H. S. (1996). Psychological predictors of school-based violence: Implications for school counselors. <u>The School Counselor, 44</u>, 35-47.

Eckstein, R., & Wallerstein, R. (1959). <u>The teaching and learning of psychotherapy</u>. NY: Basic Books.

Eugene, T. (1989). Sometimes I feel like a motherless child: The call and response for a liberational ethic of care by black feminists. In M. M. Brabeck (Ed.), <u>Who Cares? Theory, research and educational implications of the ethic of care</u> (pp. 45-62). Westport, CT: Praeger.

Gardner, H. (1993). Multiple Intelligence. New York: Basic books

Gardner, J. W. (1990). On leadership. New York: The Free Press.

Garman, N.B. (1986). Reflection, the heart of clinical supervision: A modern rationale for professional practice. Journal of Curriculum and Supervision, 2, 1-24.

Garmston, R. & Costa, A. (1984). The art of cognivitive coaching: Supervision for intelligent teaching. Sacramento, CA: California State University.

Gergen, K. J. (1985). The social constructionist movement in modern psychology. American Psychology, 40, 266-275.

Glatthorn, A.A. & Fox, L. E. (1996). Quality teaching through professional development. Thousand Oaks, CA: Corwin Press

Glatthorn, A.A. (1990). Supervisory leadership: Introduction to instructional supervision. Glenview, IL: Scott Foresman and Co.

Glickman, C.D., Gordon, S.P, Gordon, J.M. (1998). Supervision of Instruction: A developmental approach. (4th ed.) Allyn & Bacon: Nedham, MA

Goldhammer, R. (1969). Clinical supervision. NY: Holt, Rinehart & Winston

Griffin, G. (1987). Childhood predictive characteristics of aggressive adolescents. Exceptional Children, 54, 246-252.

Hart, L. A. (1983). Human brain and human learning. New York: Longman Inc.

Harth, E. (1982). Windows on the mind: Reflections on the physical basis on consciousness. New York: William Morrow and Company, Inc.

Henderson, P. & Lampe, R. (1992). "Clinical supervision of school counselors," The School Counselor. 39, 151-157.

Heppner, P. P. (1994). Dimensions that characterize supervisor interventions delivered in the context of live supervison of practicum counselors. Journal of Counseling Psychology, 41(2), 227-235.

Hogan, R. A. (1964). Issues and approaches in supervision. Psychotherapy: Theory, Research and Practice, 1, 139-141.

Holloway, E. L. (1992). Supervision: A way of teaching and learning. In S. D. Brown, & Lent, R. W. (Ed.), Handbook of Counseling Psychology (2nd ed., pp. 177-214). Toronto:John Wiley & Sons, Inc.

Holloway, E. L. (1992). Supervision: A way of teaching and learning. In S. D. Brown, & Lent, R. W. (Ed.), Handbook of Counseling Psychology (2nd ed., pp. 177-214). Toronto: John Wiley & Sons, Inc.

Holloway, E. L., & Wolleat, P. L. (1994). Supervision: The pragmatics of empowerment. Journal of Educational and Psychological Consultation, 5(1), 23-43.

Kabat-Zinn, J. (1994). Wherever you go there you are: Mindfulness meditation in everyday life. New York: Hyperion.

Kaslow, F. W., & Associates. (1977). Supervision, consultation, and staff training in the helping professions. San Francisco: Jossey-Bass Publishers.

Kelly, G. (1955). The psychology of personal constructs. New York: W.W. Norton.

Knoff, H. M. (1988). Clinical supervision, consultation, and counseling: A cmparative analysis for supervisors and other educational leaders. Journal of Curriculum and Supervision, 3(3), 240-252.

Knoff, H.M. (1988) "Clinical Supervision, consultation and counseling: A comparative analysis for supervisors and other educational leaders," Journal of Curriculum and Supervision 3, 240-252.

Knuth, R. A., & Cunningham, D. J. (1992). Tools for constructivism. In T. M. Duffy, Lowyck, J. & Jonassen, D. H. (Ed.), Designing environments for constructive learning . New York: NATO.

Kohlberg, L., & Mayer, R. (1972). Development as the aim of education: The Dewey view. Harvard Educational Review, 42, 449-496.

Kolb, D. (1984). Experiential learning: Experience as the source of learning and development. Englewood Cliffs, NJ: Prentice-Hall.

Kolb, D.A. (1981) Problem management: Learning from experience. In the Executive Mind edited by Suresy Srivasta, San Francisco: Jossey Bass.

Kouzes, J. M. & Posner, B. R. (1993). Credibility. San Francisco: Jossey Bass

Kozol, J. (1992). Savage inequalities.

Kuhn, T. S. (1970). The structure of scientific revolutions. (2nd ed.). Chicago: University of Chicago Press.

Ladany, N., Brittan-Powell, C. S., & Pannu, R. K. (1997). The influence of supervisory racial identity interaction and racial matching on the supervisory working alliance and supervisee multicultural competence. Counseling Education and Supervision, 36(4), 284-304.

Levinson, D. (1986). "A conception of adult development. American Psychologist 41(1) 3-13.

Littrell, J. M., Lee-Borden, N., & Lorenz. (1979). A developmental framework for counseling supervision. Counselor Education and Supervision, 19, 129-136.

Loganbill, C. R., Hardy, C.V. & Delworth, U. (1982). Supervision: A Conceptual Model. The Counseling Psychologist, 10(1), 3-42.

Mahon, B. R., & Altmann, H. A. (1977). Skill Training: Cautions and recommendations. Counselor Education and Supervision, 17, 42-50.

Maslow, A. (1954).Motivation and personality. NY: Harper and Row.

Maturana, H. R. V. (1987). The tree of knowledge: The biological roots of human understanding. Boston: New Science Library.

Mayo, E. (1933). The human problem of an industrial civiliaztion. MacMillan: NY

McCutcheon, G. (1995). Developing the curriculum NY: Longman

McGregor, D. (1960). The human side of enterprise. McGraw Hill: NY

Mezirow, J. (1994). Understanding transformation theory. Adult Education Quarterly, 44(4), 222-44.

Myers, J. (1993). Social Psychology. (3rd ed.). New York: McGraw Hill.

Myers, J. (1993). Social Psychology. (3rd ed.). New York: McGraw Hill.

National Coalition of State Juvenile Justice Advisory Groups, (1993).

Neufeldt, S. A., Karno, M. P., & Nelson, M. L. (1996). A qualitative study of experts' conceptualization of supervisee reflectivity. Journal of counseling psychology, 43(1), 3-9.

Neufeldt, S. A., Karno, M. P., & Nelson, M. L. (1996). A qualitative study of experts' conceptualization of supervisee reflectivity. Journal of counseling psychology, 43(1), 3-9.

Noddings, N. (1991). Stories in dialogue: Caring and interpersonal reasoning. In C. Witherell, & Noddings, N. (Ed.), Stories Lives Tell (pp. 157-170). New York: Teachers College Press.

Perry, W. G. (1970). Forms of intellectual and ethical development in the college years. New York: Holt, Rinehart & Wilson.

Peterson, M.D. (1960). The Jefferson image in the american mind. NY: Oxford University Press.

Piaget, J. (1970). Structuralism. New York: Basic Books.

Rabinowitz, F., Heppner, P.P. & Roehlke, H.J. (1986). Descriptive study of process and outcome variables of supervision over time. Journal of Counseling Psychology, 33(3), 292-300.

Ross, D. D. (1989). First steps in developing a reflective approach. Journal of Teacher Education, 40(2), 22-30.

Rotter, J. B. (1954). Social learning and clinical psychology. Englewood Cliffs, NJ: Prentice Hall.

Russel, B. W., Alfred North. (1910). Principia Mathematica. (2nd ed.). (Vol. 1). Cambridge: Cambridge University Press.

Russell, R. K., Crimmings, A.M. & Lent, R.W. (1984). Counselor Training and supervision: Theory and Research. New York: Wiley.

Russell-Chapin, L., Lyman, L., Sherman, N., Castle, S., Berube, L., Ryback, C., & Smith, C. (1996) "Gaps in counselor role perceptions: The need for collaboration," ICA Quarterly, 42, 34-50.

Schnarch, D. M. (1991). Constructing the sexual cruciable. New York: W. W. Norton & Company.

Schon, D. A. (1987). Educating the reflective practitioner: Toward a new design for teaching and learning in the professions. San Francisco: Jossey-Bass.

Schon, D. A. (1987). Educating the reflective practitioner: Toward a new design for teaching and learning in the professions. San Francisco: Jossey-Bass.

Selman, R. L. (1980). The growth of interpersonal undestanding. New York: Academic Press.

Senge, P. M. (1990). The fifth discipline: The art & practice of the learning organization. New York: Currency Doubleday.

Sergiovanni, T. J. & Starratt, R. J. (1998). Supervision a redefinition. (6th ed.). NY: McGraw-Hill.

Sergiovanni, T. J. & Starratt, R. J. (1998). Supervision a redefinition. (6th ed.). NY: McGraw-Hill.

Sergiovanni, T.J. (1998). Moral Leadership. San Francisco, CA: Jossey Bass,

Sexton, T. L., & Whiston, S. C. (1994). The status of the counseling relationship: An empirical review, theoretical implications and research directions. The Counseling Psychologist, 22(1), 7-70.

Sexton, T. L., & Whiston, S. C. (1994). The status of the counseling relationship: An empirical review, theoretical implications and research directions. The Counseling Psychologist, 22(1), 7-70.

Sheldrake, R. (1981). A new science of life. Las Angeles: Jeremy Tarcher.

Shulman, L. (1987). Knowledge and teaching: Foundations of the new reform. Harvard Educational Review, 57(1), 1-22.

Simon, F., Stierlin, H., & Wynne, L. (1985). The language of family therapy; A systemic vocabulary and sourcebook. New York: Family Process Press.

Skovholt, T. (1993). Supervision of Beginning and Advanced Graduate Students of Counseling Trainees. Journal of Counseling and Development, 71, 396-405.

Skovholt, T. (1993). Supervision of Beginning and Advanced Graduate Students of Counseling Trainees. Journal of Counseling and Development, 71, 396-405.

Skovholt, T., Cognetta, P., Ye, G., & King, L. (1997). Violence prevention strategies of inner-city student experts. Professional School Counselor.

Srebalus, D. J., Schwartz, J. L., Vaughan, R.V., & Tunick, R.H. (1996). Youth violence in rural schools: Counselor perceptions and treatment resources. School Counselor, 44.

Starratt, R. J. (1993). The Drama of Leadership. London: The Falmer Press.

Stoltenberg, C. D. & Delworth, (1987). Developmental supervisiomn: A training model for counselors and psychotherapists. San Francisco: Jossey Bass.

Stoltenberg, C. D. (1981). Approaching supervision from a developmental perspective: The counselor complexity model. Journal of Counseling Psychology, 28, 59-65.

Stuessy, C. L., & Naizer, G. L. (1996). Reflection and problem solving: Integrating methods of teaching mathematics and science. School Science and Mathematics, 96(4), 170-177.

Tracey, T. J., Ellickson, J. L. & Sherry, P. (1989). Reactance in relation to different supervisory environments and counselor development. Journal of counseling Psychology, 36, 336-344.

Tremmel, R. (1993). Zen and the art of reflection practice in teacher education. Harvard Educational Review, 63(4), 434-458.

Van Manen, M. (1977). Linking ways of knowing with ways of being practical. Curriculum Inquiry, 6, 205-228.

Ward, C., & House, R. (1998). Counseling supervision: A reflective model. Counselor Education and Supervision, 38(1), 23-33.

Ward, C., & House, R. (1999). On-site counseling supervision experience of school counseling interns. Manuscript submitted, Counselor Education and Supervision.

Watkins, E. C. (1995). Psychotherapy supervisor and supervisee: Developmetnal models and research nine years later. Clinical Psychology Review, 15(7), 647-680.

Weakland, J. H. J., L. (1990). Working briefly with reluctant clients: Child protective services as example. Family Therapy Case Studies, 5, 51-68.

Wertheimer, M. (Ed.). (1923). On objects as immediately given to consciousness. Cambridge, MA: Harvard University Press.

Wheatley, M. (1992). Leadership and the new science. San Francisco: Berrett Koehler.

Wheatley, M. (1992). Leadership and the new science. San Francisco: Berret-Koehler Publishers, Inc.

Worthen, V., & McNeill, B. W. (1996). A phenomenological investigation of "good" supervision events. Journal of Counseling Psychology, 43(1), 25-34.

Worthen, V., & McNeill, B. W. (1996). A phenomenological investigation of "good" supervision events. Journal of Counseling Psychology, 43(1), 25-34.

Worthington, E. L. (1984). Empirical investigation of supervision of counselors as they gain experience. Journal of Counseling Psychology, 31, 63-75.

Yogev, S. (1982). "An eclectic model of supervision: A developmental model for psychotherapy students," Professional Psychologist, 236-243

Index

MELLEN STUDIES IN EDUCATION